PANZER III

**Panzerkampfwagen III
Ausf A to N (SdKfz 141)**

First published in February 2017.

A catalogue record for this book is available from the British Library.

ISBN 978 085733 827 3

Library of Congress control no. 2015948112

Published by Haynes Publishing,
Sparkford, Yeovil,
Somerset BA22 7JJ, UK.
Tel: 01963 440635
Int. tel: +44 1963 440635
Website: www.haynes.com

Haynes North America Inc.,
859 Lawrence Drive, Newbury Park,
California 91320, USA.

Printed in Malaysia

Commissioning editor: Jonathan Falconer
Copy editor: Bourchier Ltd
Proof reader: Penny Housden
Indexer: Peter Nicholson
Page design: James Robertson

PANZER III

Panzerkampfwagen III
Ausf A to N (SdKfz 141)

Owners' Workshop Manual

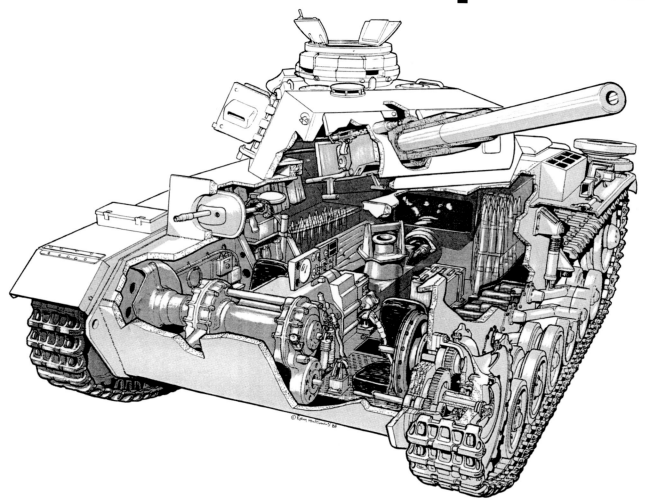

An insight into the design, construction and operation of the
German Army's Second World War medium battle tank

Dick Taylor and Mike Hayton

Contents

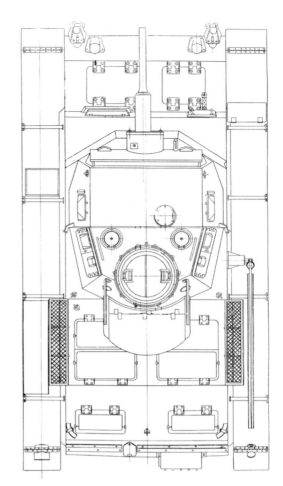

OPPOSITE Italy: a Panzer III Ausf N is maintained by its crew out of action, with the turret traversed so that the gun is over the engine decks. This tank, number 121, has the turret Schürzen fitted and the turret smoke grenade dischargers are loaded ready for the next combat.
(Bundesarchiv Bild 101I-308-0799Q-11A)

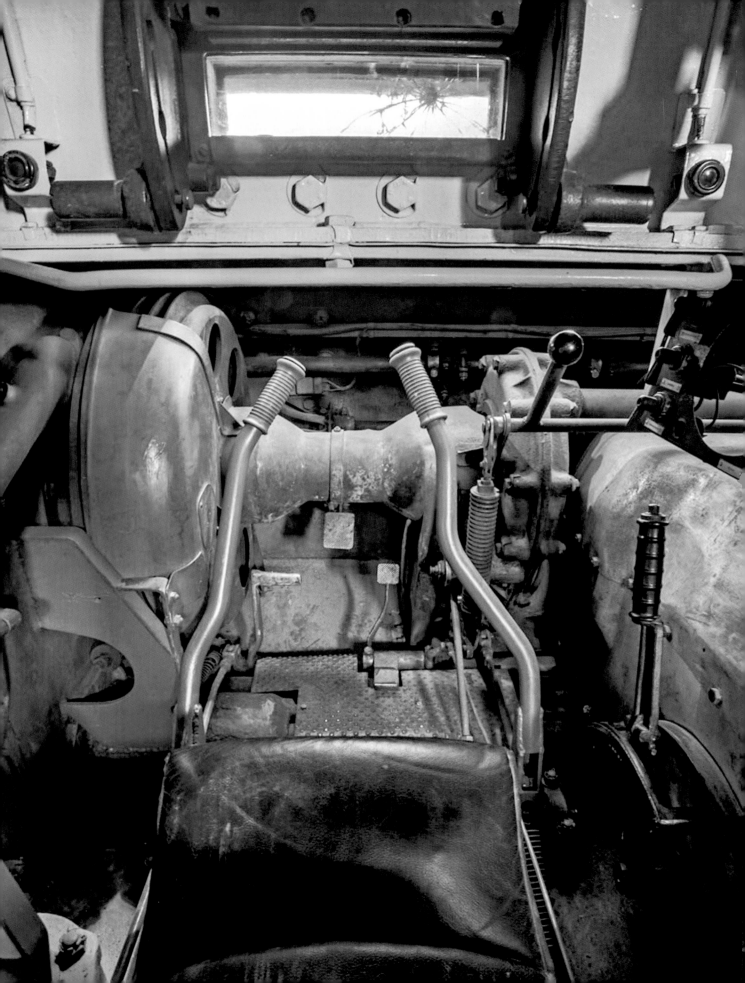

Foreword

David Willey, Curator, Tank Museum

This volume in the Haynes series on tanks looks at one of the workhorse vehicles of the German panzer force in the Second World War – the Panzerkampfwagen III or SdKfz 141. Later interest in heavy German armour has filled the bookshelves and forums with material on the Panther, Tiger and King Tiger – and this tends to overshadow the earlier war period of glory for German tanks such as the Panzers III and IV.

As with so much tank history, there is a tendency for myth to obscure the facts, something particularly prevalent with German tank history where some myths still widely believed directly relate to the German propaganda of the time. The official German history of the 1940 campaign is called *The Legend of Blitzkrieg* and though it was written in 1995, still new histories appear telling of brilliant German tanks designed to meet a faultless, long-prepared and cunning German battle plan. The facts show that Hitler took his limited steel production away from making tanks in 1939 to manufacture more artillery shells, as he saw the forthcoming battle more like a First World War siege. His conversion to tanks after their success in 1940 gave him a belief in their invincibility – and an inflated belief in his own abilities as an armour commander. Recent economic histories of the Third Reich have also shown how – just like today – armies rarely get the equipment they want or require – but what is affordable at the time.

Designed originally to carry an armour-piercing gun and to be the main battle tank of the German tank arm, its sister vehicle, the support tank or Panzer IV, was to carry a larger gun but be made in smaller numbers to accompany troop attacks – three companies of Panzer III tanks to one of Panzer IV. Both tanks were to be fitted with radios – a feature that may seem common sense today, but one that was to help give German tanks a tactical advantage against the better-armoured or -armed tanks they were to meet in combat.

In due course the Panzer IV showed more potential to be up-gunned, so the original role of the Panzer III was taken over by the Panzer IV. Plans were made to create a more uniform vehicle – almost a hybrid between the Panzers III and IV – to ease supply and training requirements, but the idea was finally dropped in the autumn of 1944.

Dick Taylor has written two very successful volumes on British tanks of the post-war era in this Haynes series and here he enters the much-debated topic of German tanks. This volume gives a balanced insight into a tank that was associated with the initial years of German success, with a plethora of new images and the perception of a man who has spent many years on tanks.

David Willey
Bovington, 1 October 2016

ACKNOWLEDGEMENTS

Particular thanks must go to: David Willey (the originator of this project), Stuart Wheeler, Matt Sampson and Steve Malley, all of the Tank Museum, Bovington; Col (Retd) Stephen White MBE; all the staff of the Archive & Library at the Tank Museum, particularly Jonathan Holt for his diligence and patience; the Joint Services Command and Staff College Library, Shrivenham; the National Archives, Kew.

Chapter One

The Panzer III story

The Panzer III became a symbol of German success in the early war years, but its development and production was far from simple. Germany had to build up the skills and capacity for tank production in a country that had been banned from producing tanks by the Versailles Peace Treaty and whose automobile industry lagged far behind in scale when compared to Britain and France.

OPPOSITE Panzer IIIs advancing into Latvia in June 1941 at the spearhead of Operation Barbarossa. At this stage of the war the Panzer III was Germany's main battle tank, but within a year it would be exposed as under-gunned and lacking in armour, and production ceased in 1943. Despite this, the chassis was used as the basis of many variants, including a successful family of assault guns. *(Bundesarchiv)*

Background

The appearance of the very first Panzer III in 1937 marked a turning point for the newly formed *Panzerwaffe*, the German armoured force.[1] At last they had a genuine battle tank, designed and built in Germany, and one which would provide excellent service for the time remaining to the Third Reich. During the First World War the Germans had been both strategically and tactically surprised by the appearance of British tanks on the Somme in September 1916, and had never managed to

catch up. Although they were able to field their own design of tank in 1918, the ungainly A7V, they never came close to competing with the Allies and the best tanks that they operated were those captured from their enemies. This left a lasting impression on many of the officers involved, and, having seen the potential of this new weapon of war, they were determined to exploit it in the future. In order to understand how the Panzer III came about and why it took the form that it did, we must first examine the context in which it was built; we will start with the Armistice that brought the First World War to an end. Crucially, we must acknowledge from the outset that the roots of German rearmament and the creation of the German tank arm pre-dated the rise of Hitler by a number of years. It is probably fair to say that most laymen believe that German tank design and production started with Hitler and the Panzer I, and do not realise just how much work on developing tanks had been done before he came to power, and which laid the groundwork for the legends that still surround them. Had German tank development only started after Hitler came to power, we can be quite certain that the *Panzerwaffe* would not have turned out the way it did. Despite this, we must also turn our attention to how rearmament occurred in Germany under Hitler, focusing on the decisions that affected the plans to produce a tank-centric army, and explain how the desires

---

1 Throughout this book, the fuller German designation of *Panzerkampfwagen* (Pz Kpfw) III will be abbreviated to Panzer III – anathema for the purists, but easier for the majority. During the Second World War the British tended to refer to the tank as the German Mk III.

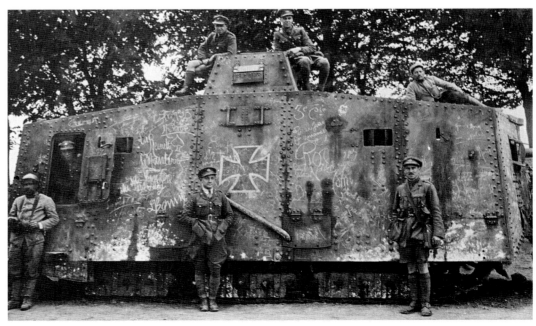

of the panzer generals were often thwarted by interference from the politicians. Most importantly, we should consider how the Panzer III developed over its lifetime and whether or not it should go down in history as a success.

Central to this book is the beautifully restored Panzer III Ausf L which is part of the collection at the Tank Museum, Bovington. The tank was built by MAN in Nürnberg in June 1942, bearing the *Fahrgestell* number 74375. It was shipped to Benghazi via Naples on 18 July on the SS *Lerica*. By the end of July it had been issued to the 7th Light Company of Pz Regt 8 in 15th Pz Div. It served at the Battle of Alam el Halfa a month later where it was captured in good condition. Because it was a new model with the long 50mm gun, it was shipped back to the School of Tank Technology in Chertsey for detailed examination and was eventually presented to the Tank Museum in 1951. It required extensive and expert restoration to return it to the superb condition that it is in today, and the story of that restoration project, as told here by the workshop manager Mike Hayton, allows us to look into the design of the tank at a level of detail that plans and period photographs cannot compete with.

German tank development between the wars

The Reichswehr and secret German rearmament

The terms of the Treaty of Versailles signed on Saturday 28 June 1919 (coincidentally exactly five years to the day after the assassination of Archduke Franz Ferdinand) limited the total German army to no more than 100,000 men, in a maximum of seven infantry and three cavalry divisions. In order to prevent the Reichswehr (as the new armed forces were called, literally meaning the Empire Defence Force) from being able to create reserves by rotating personnel through the force, its soldiers had to serve for a minimum of 12 years, and

officers for 25.[2] Specifically relating to our subject, Germany was forbidden to possess tanks or even armoured cars, and the General Staff and the War College were both abolished.[3] The air force was totally banned and the navy restricted to 15,000 sailors. These and the other clauses – there were over 400 – are often quoted now, with the wisdom of hindsight, to be among the causes of the Second World War; in fact they were also seen by many at the time in the same light. Lloyd George said that the treaty was more of a 'hell-peace than a heaven-peace', and that 'we shall have to do the whole thing over again in twenty five years at three times the cost'. Foch famously stated that 'This is not a peace. It is an armistice for twenty years.' They were both correct.

For the first few years of the new German state, there was little chance that the terms of the treaty could be broken, as Allied troops were stationed within Germany and the Inter-Allied Military Control Commission (IMCC) used spies and informants to keep an eye on Germany from within. By 1927 these forces had been withdrawn and the senior officers of the Reichswehr had already started to look for opportunities to bypass the terms of the treaty and to begin to rebuild the army in a more modern form.[4] By this time the Allies

---

2 This was only partially successful – it led to fewer men entering the army, but those who did were hugely experienced by the time expansion was begun. General Hans von Seeckt also managed to have about 60% of its strength as officers and senior NCOs, in preparation for a future rapid expansion.

3 The wording of Article 169 forbade 'the manufacture and importation into Germany of armoured cars, tanks, and all other similar constructions of war'.

4 In a 1920 amendment, the Reichswehr was authorised to acquire 105 armoured troop carriers, which they interpreted as armoured cars. Models were built by Benz, Erhardt and Daimler, and all featured front and rear steering, a characteristic that became common in later German armoured cars.

were taking a less aggressive stance towards Germany, which had joined the League of Nations in 1926 and formally renounced war as an instrument of policy when it signed the Kellogg–Briand Pact of 1928. This set the stage for the Reichswehr to plan for secret expansion and to look for ways of re-equipping itself with modern weapons, with tanks high on the shopping list. It must always be remembered that Germany was not able at this stage to conduct this openly, and therefore the start of the much-vaunted German tank-building programme started both slowly and secretly.

One element of the programme, and which was later to relate directly to the weapons with which Germany's tanks were to be armed, was that of anti-tank defence. Germany had been on the receiving end of the majority of the tank attacks made during the war, and, not surprisingly, took the issue of anti-tank defence very seriously. As well as developing anti-tank mines the Reichswehr identified the need for a better infantry anti-tank weapon than the clumsy and largely ineffective 13mm rifle used in the trenches, and one which would also remove the need to rely on field artillery to destroy tanks. Although tank armour had not developed much since the end of the war – with a thickness of only around 15mm being the norm – it was decided to develop a small anti-tank gun to be used by the infantry, which would be light and easily portable by a small gun crew, and yet which would have enough hitting power to penetrate the tanks

then in service. Design work started in 1924, and by 1928 a horse-drawn 37mm weapon had entered service. This would lead to the development of a smaller carriage with rubber-tyred wheels able to be moved easily by an infantry crew of four, which entered service in 1934 as the PaK 35/36.[5] As we shall see, this was developed – not without controversy – into the first gun used on the Panzer III, the 37mm KwK 36.[6]

Even before this, in the early 1920s the Reichswehr began to study the uses of armoured warfare in future conflicts, and the active support of the army commander-in-chief General Hans von Seeckt was crucial in pushing forward the new doctrine. Von Seeckt, who called himself an 'unpolitical soldier', was one of a group of almost unknown officers who were the true fathers of the panzer arm. The banned General Staff was de facto in existence, hidden within the operations department (known as T1) of the *Truppenamt*, or troop office, and a separate Weapons Office was also established. Staff officers entrusted with the responsibility of developing doctrine spent a lot of time examining how the other nations were developing their armoured forces, and reading the dozens of articles and theories prompted by the invention of the new weapon. In most cases the tank was seen as an infantry support weapon, the role it had been invented for, and many believed that this approach constrained

5 *PanzerAbwehrKanone*, or anti-tank cannon.
6 *KampfWagenKanone*, or combat vehicle cannon.

RIGHT The small and light PaK 35/36 was the basis for the first gun fitted to the Panzer III, which was adequate when first mounted but soon came to be referred to as the 'door-knocker'. *(All photos from author's collection unless credited otherwise)*

the development of it as a weapon in its own right. German officers seemed to have been more impressed with those far-sighted individuals who saw the enormous potential of the tank in restoring mobility to the battlefield, and who wrote passionately of the tank as the new weapon of decision, combining the manoeuvre of the cavalry with the firepower of the artillery, with the added bonus of protection. As well as studying international doctrine as a precursor to formulating their own, the Reichswehr looked around for places where it could develop tank technology in secret, and found the answers in two unlikely places: Sweden and the USSR.

Two prototypes of a light tank called the *Leicht Kampfwagen* I (LK I or light combat vehicle) had been made in 1918. A development called the LK II then followed, but the end of the war prevented a large order from being started. However, after the war the Swedish government secretly bought enough LK II components for the AB Landsverk company to build ten tanks which they called Strv Model 1921; assisting them in this was the senior German tank designer, Josef Vollmer. Also in 1921 the premier German armaments company Krupp managed to acquire the Swedish Bofors company, and used the cover of this to send experts and engineers to maintain and develop their skills. These examples show how both countries were

ABOVE LEFT The monocled General Hans von Seeckt, commander of the Reichswehr until 1926. He was central in starting German efforts to rearm with a range of modern weapons, including tanks. He saw his core task as preparing the Reichswehr for future expansion into a much larger and more capable force; Hitler later suppressed his biography, probably in an effort to claim credit for von Seeckt's achievements.

ABOVE A Swedish M21, based on the German LK II design of 1918.

prepared to work closely and in secret. The Germans were quick to seize the opportunity of assisting the Swedes, in part as a means of accessing foreign currency but mainly to improve their understanding of tank design and production.[7] Sweden was also happy to export large quantities of high-grade iron ore, necessary for steel production, to Germany, but as we shall see supply could never match demand, particularly in the 1930s when Germany's foreign currency reserves and therefore purchasing power began to run low.

Meanwhile, in Germany, thought was given to how best to develop doctrine and tactics for tanks without actually possessing any, and indeed with no likelihood of doing so for a number of years. The solution was simple, if perhaps a trifle Heath Robinson. Units were instructed to make representative tanks out of wood and canvas, and fit them over cars and

---

7   The pre-eminent German tank general Heinz Guderian drove a tank for the first time while in Sweden.

ABOVE German units in the 1931 exercise season training with tanks made from wood and canvas.

other light vehicles in order to represent tanks on exercises. In some cases they were made of cardboard and were light enough to mount on bicycles – or even on small wheels propelled by soldier power. By doing this they were not in breach of the Treaty of Versailles, but in any case it was kept as quiet as possible. What had to be kept absolutely secret was the development of actual tanks. Von Seeckt had tried as early as 1921 to establish co-operation with the embryonic USSR, but the war was too fresh in the memory and he was rebuffed. Despite this, the Reichswehr realised that the best hope of developing new weapons in secret lay in the east, and continued to push for liaison between the two erstwhile enemies who had one thing in common: they were international pariahs.

The Reichswehr system of obtaining new weapons was for the appropriate Weapons Office to issue a specification and

RIGHT This poster reads: 'The German Army uses dummy tanks to accustom its troops to anti-tank defence.' Not surprisingly there is no mention of using them to develop tank doctrine.

Zur Gewöhnung der Truppe an die Abwehr der Waffe verwendet das deutsche Heer Tankattrappen.

TANK

a development contract to two or three commercial firms, which would then develop prototypes that could be tested in competition with the rivals. After the trials, the General Staff – in the guise of the *Truppenamt* – made the final decision which, if any, of the prototypes should be further developed or put into (at this stage limited) production. This system guaranteed that due to the intense competition for army contracts, the companies had to work at the top of their game and thus the standard of weapons was able to be improved. Unlike in many armies, using new technology was the name of the game, and while conservative elements did persist, particularly with regard to cavalry, the general desire to develop and employ cutting-edge technology was well in advance of that found within the countries who had won the war.

In May 1925, over seven years before Hitler came to power, the first development contract was issued for genuine tanks. The firms of Daimler, Rheinmetall and Krupp were requested to build two 16–20-ton tanks each, sometimes referred to as *Armeewagen 20*. These were to have an engine of 260–280hp, capable of producing a top speed of 40kph. This was, for the time, an amazing specification, asking for such a powerful engine and top speed; in comparison, the in-service Medium II tank in the British army used a 90hp engine giving a top speed of about 20kph. The *Armeewagen 20* would mount 14mm of armour,[8] a standard amount for the period, but would be armed with a 75mm gun in a rotating turret, plus two or three machine guns, and it would carry a radio. All in all, this was a big ask for a country with limited experience of tanks. Because of the need for secrecy, the *Armeewagen* designation was dropped and the tank was referred to by the camouflage name of *Grosstraktor* or heavy tractor, as tracked agricultural machines were permitted under the Treaty of Versailles. Daimler designed the *Grosstraktor* I, Krupp the II and Rheinmetall the III. All six were constructed at Rheinmetall's Unterlüss factory in northern Germany between August 1928 and July the following year. Each of the firms used the same engine,[9] but experimented with different gearbox,

8   In theory – the prototypes were all built of mild steel.
9   Sources differ here: one states a BMW 250hp unit was used, another that 260hp Daimlers were employed.

steering and suspension types. All featured small roadwheels, but with different methods of shock absorption, and it was in the area of suspension that the first models of the Panzer III were to differ, as working out which system was the best proved to be difficult. It should be emphasised that in this period computer models were not able to predict how new technologies might perform in reality, and so there was no substitute for the trial-and-error method which was widely used. For example, the German welding expert Herr Schieffelbein carried out between 5,000 and 6,000 experiments to determine the optimum welding electrode to use with armour plate. Demonstrating how forward-thinking the Germans were, it was originally ordered that in addition to the futuristic specification already noted, all the designs should be amphibious. Owing to the technical difficulties in achieving this, however, the requirement was dropped in the early 1930s. The *Grosstraktor* programme was an important leap forward for the Germans – it was ambitious but it produced workable designs from which much was learned and which would be used in the near future. Additionally, it marked the first foray into genuine tank design for the legendary Ferdinand Porsche, who was Daimler's chief designer.

The next development contract was given to the same three firms in July 1928 for a smaller tank camouflaged as a *Leichttraktor* or light tractor. For reasons unknown, Daimler pulled out, leaving just four prototypes to be completed. As they were simpler and smaller, they only took about 18 months to design and produce. The chassis was intended to become a multi-purpose design, able to be used as the basis for a family of different vehicles. Although only in the light tank category, it would be armed with a very capable 37mm gun in a revolving turret. This tank was designed to fulfil a different role to the heavy tractor, which was seen as being used for infantry support – hence the larger gun with a bigger HE shell. The 37mm weapon was the standard anti-tank gun, and so the light tractor was designed to engage enemy tanks. In an important advance in armour technology – indeed in what was probably *the* most important advance made by anyone between the two world wars – the German vehicles all featured welded armour

plate. Welded armour offered significant advantages over the traditional riveted construction: it was lighter, the joints were stronger and the crews were better protected as they were not subject to the rivets becoming secondary projectiles if hit.

In 1928 Lieutenant Colonel Oswald Lutz of the Inspectorate of Motor Troops, who was a key figure in the procurement of the tractors, also requested designs for multi-wheeled armoured cars, with contracts awarded to Büssing, Magirus and Daimler. (It may be that Daimler felt better suited to armoured car design rather than tracked tanks, and this would explain them pulling out of the *Leichttraktor* project.) Although a ten-wheeled version was unsuccessfully trialled, the six- and eight-wheeled versions showed promise and were the forerunners of the large armoured cars that became famous during the Second World

ABOVE A *Grosstraktor* in a garish, multi-colour camouflage scheme negotiates an obstacle during trials. *(TM 1755/C2)*

LEFT Ferdinand Porsche, Daimler's chief designer who oversaw the design of their version of the *Grosstraktor*. Although many of his tank designs were overcomplicated failures, his (plagiarised) torsion bar suspension system was successfully adopted on the Panzer III Ausf E.

War. Thus by the early 1930s not only had the Germans conducted a number of technically advanced and ambitious design studies, they had also discovered which companies were best suited to which vehicle type. The *Grosstraktor* designs in particular had been improved through three main configurations, reducing the crew size and improving the armour thickness, plus introducing such features as side escape hatches. This knowledge was to be used directly in the designs for the next German medium tank, one of which was to emerge in the future as the Panzer III.

An important point to note here with both types of *Traktor* is how similar they were in many respects, despite being produced by different companies who were commercial competitors. Supervising the efforts of all three firms was a certain Captain Hans Pirner; this indicates that the German military authorities did not give complete free rein to the companies, but insisted on certain common aspects of design – for example with the light tractor, that the engine must be in the front and the turret to the rear. This gives us an early clue to the answer of an often-asked question – why did the Panzers III and IV look so very similar, despite being designed by different companies? The implication is that the German army was more closely involved in the design and development process than, for instance, in the UK, where the companies had a much greater freedom in meeting the specifications that they were given. We should also be aware that Germany, despite becoming a dictatorship in 1933, was not a totalitarian society in the sense that the USSR was. As we shall shortly discuss, it still functioned as a capitalist economy, dominated by large engineering firms who needed to make a profit for their shareholders.

Training in Russia

In 1922 Germany and Russia signed the Treaty of Rapallo, which as well as trying to normalise relations after the First World War, included a secret clause that was the basis for increased military co-operation between two states who were pariahs in the collective mind of the victors of the First World War. This led to the Soviets agreeing in October 1926 that the Germans could make use of a 6-square-mile training area near to the Kargopol barracks on the Kama river, in the desolate Kazan region about 500km east of Moscow.[10] As well as providing a large area in which to test new vehicles, around a dozen selected German officers would attend year-long technical courses at the base. The existence of the school, along with another three used elsewhere in the USSR for other purposes, was such a sensitive issue that its existence was kept from all but a handful of senior politicians within the government, although the secret did leak and was even exposed by the *Manchester Guardian*. The officers at the school wore civilian clothing (and on occasion Soviet uniforms), and had to resign from the Reichswehr while attending the courses there, where they were officially classed as tourists.

Courses started in March 1929, with the first six tanks, the heavy tractors, secretly shipped from Germany by July. Classes contained a mix of Russian and German officers, and covered both technical aspects and tactics; the students were able to get their hands on some foreign vehicles, including British Carden-Loyd tankettes, which were subsequently influential

---

10 As well as being on the river of the same name, the name Kama was chosen as a contraction of Kazan and Malbrandt (aka Mahlbrand), the German officer who selected the site and who was the first commandant. The Soviets called the whole programme TEKO, a short acronym for 'Technical Courses of the Society for Defence, Aviation and Construction of Chemical Weapons'.

in the design of Germany's first genuine light tank, the Panzer I. The Germans were fairly senior, mostly lieutenant colonels, who would go on to become important champions of the new panzer arm. Among the German officers on the first course was Wilhelm von Thoma, later to command the Afrika Korps. However, the most important figure for our story was not a student but one of the instructors, Captain Ernst Volckheim. Virtually (and undeservingly) unknown, he was critical to German tank development between the wars. Volckheim was a deep-thinking soldier with experience of tank combat in the First World War who immediately grasped the significance of the new weapon. Heinz Guderian mentioned him only once in his (extremely self-serving) memoirs. The experience of that war did not lead Guderian to realise immediately the potential of the tank, and he even fought against his first appointment in a technical role in 1922. However, Guderian eventually came to understand the possibilities and, with the dedication so typical of a late convert, applied himself to developing tanks for German use. But Volckheim deserves to be much better known.

As well as advocating the fitment of radios to all tanks – at a time when many experts believed it was technically impossible to transmit or receive effectively from a moving vehicle – Volckheim immersed himself in reading articles from other nations, and then writing his own, developing his own brand of armoured warfare. It was from this comparatively low-ranking officer that much of Germany's armoured doctrine derived, and with it, the specification for the tanks necessary to make it a reality. For example, in the First World War the most successful German artillery piece was the famous 77mm; however, while at Kama, the Germans decided to concentrate on two calibres for future development: 37mm as the anti-tank gun, and 75mm as the new artillery field gun. The desire to standardise led to the adoption of 75mm as a calibre for tank-mounted support weapons, as well as the 37mm first as an anti-tank gun for the infantry and then as a tank gun.[11] Another important

lesson learned from the experiments conducted at this time at Kama was the need for the tank commander to be placed in the main turret of the tank, and to be provided with good vision equipment giving him all-round observation.

Another form of control was even more important. In 1929 the engineers at Kama managed, for the first time, to mount two relatively small radios in each tank, making command and control – which allowed tactical orders and reports to be made in real time – a practical proposition. This concept of thinking ahead is amply demonstrated by the fact that the Reichswehr had, as early as 1922, required each tank to be built with space for a radio mounting, despite the technology not yet being available. Intriguingly, although for most of the Second World War the German firm Telefunken were the leading radio supplier almost to the point of monopoly, in the 1920s and early 1930s most advances came through the German Lorenz subsidiary of a US company, IT&TC, which had developed a series of ruggedised VHF radios for commercial applications – including Amazonian exploration. Lorenz subsequently developed their elegant solutions with increasing Reichswehr interest and support, and they used the experience to build the *Funkgerät* FuG 5 radios later used on the Panzer III.

From 1933 Germany felt that it was no longer necessary to continue using the

---

11 Although millimetres are used here, the Germans generally referred to larger weapons by centimetres; hence the 75mm would be referred to as a 7.5cm. Again, the purists will be chewing their carpets at this point. …

secret school, and closed it, transferring its activities back inside Germany, thereby openly conducting tank design and development for the first time since 1918. The new Chancellor Hitler, at least partly for ideological reasons, was also keen that all advances should be made inside Germany and probably played a part in the school's closure.

Hitler comes to power

When Hitler came to power on 30 January 1933 he was determined to continue the rearmament work already conducted by the military, although with much more direct political control than had previously been the case. His intent to become closely involved in military matters was signalled only four days later, when he addressed the senior Reichswehr officers on 3 February. He formed a close alliance with General Blomberg, appointing him Defence Minister and commander of the Wehrmacht on 27 April 1933. Hitler often referred to a policy of *wiederwehrhaftmachung*, meaning national remilitarisation – so much more than mere rearmament; this implied the physical and psychological preparation of the whole state for a future war. On 9 February 1933 Hitler stated that 'Billions of marks are necessary for rearmament … the future of Germany depends exclusively on the rebuilding of the armed forces. Every other task must take second place to rearmament.'

Initially the rearmament focus was firmly on improving defensive measures, and for good reason. During the late 1920s the preoccupation of the Reichswehr generals had been the possibility of a war with Poland; every one of the many war games that they conducted had concluded that Germany would be crushed by the Poles. The first priority for Hitler, therefore, was to reverse the results so that Germany could not be defeated; only later did the direction move towards ensuring a victory. One of the possible solutions was to use increased mechanisation, which of course included the use of tanks. This amounted to what one commentator described as delivering 'the greatest possible military efficiency with the smallest possible investment in materiel and personnel.' The problem was that armoured doctrine was still in its infancy, and despite all the visions of massed armoured formations sweeping all before them, it was not clear to anyone that tanks could be used in a purely defensive role. It was therefore only once Germany was confident that her neighbours could not militarily defeat her she was able to shift attention – and therefore priority – to more offensive and aggressive methods.

By mid-1934 59% of German engineering and vehicle manufacture and 56% of the iron and steel industries were reserved for military use only. In the same year the army had been reorganised to include a new command structure for the tank forces, the *Kommando der Panzertruppen*, which was given to Oswald Lutz. More developmental contracts were placed: the light Panzer I entered production in 1934 and the enlarged Panzer II followed in 1935. Even before the Panzers III and IV were ordered, it

RIGHT The Krupp-designed LaS tractor was disguised as an agricultural vehicle but the chassis was used for early driver training and developed into the Panzer I light tank. It utilised the rear engine with front drive sprocket and transmission that was a feature of German tanks. *(Tank Museum)*

is important to note that the first four German tanks shared many features; each newer and larger tank was in many ways a scaled-up version of the previous one. An examination of the turret and hull fronts will make this clear, and all featured a front transmission and drive sprockets, characteristics that will be examined in more detail in Chapter 3.

Hitler's control over German business, and in particular the larger companies, was crucial to the form that German tank development took, with the state able to exert much more control over the weapons it received than anywhere else in the world except the USSR. In part, this was because the weakening of the companies following the Wall Street Crash in 1929 had led to state bailouts that placed many of the companies under at least partial governmental control. Additionally, as Hitler's regime grew in strength, it imposed controls over the functioning of big business that would have been impossible in a normal capitalist economy. The Nazi state increasingly interfered with the production of weapons, strengthening the trend that had started in the days of the Reichswehr; the companies did not have a completely free hand in designing to a specification, but were closely supervised by Wehrmacht officers who had the power to insist on design changes. This is a major reason why the Panzers III and IV, designed and built by different firms, looked so very similar but shared surprisingly little commonality in major components. What could have been a huge strength in terms of standardisation became a weakness. This was in part due to a German obsession with new technology for its own sake – which was encouraged by Hitler – and partly because of the continuing use of competitive design contracts. These produced prototype tanks that were often very similar, with the production contract awarded to the winner of the trials. It was only subsequently, when the service tank was made, that standardisation failed; each firm built components to their own design, with little reference or co-ordination with other firms building similar models. Funnily enough, the highest level of standardisation was achieved with the smaller components – screws, bolts, washers, etc. British reports from just after the war were very complimentary about how

ABOVE The Panzer II was another light tank, armed only with a 20mm cannon and machine gun, but again it showed many of the design features and general layout that would be carried forward for the Panzers III and IV.

standardised the Germans were in this respect, opining that they were much more advanced than either the UK or USA.

Hitler envisaged building up Germany's armed forces in two stages. Firstly, secret rearmament was to continue until Germany reached the point where it would be able to reliably defend itself against its neighbours and therefore need not fear invasion. This lasted until 1935, when rearmament became more open. Conscription was reintroduced on 16 March that year, shredding the last vestiges of the Treaty of Versailles. Thereafter, the second phase involved increasing quantity and quality, until Germany was in a position to go to war where and when it chose. Between 1935 and 1938, 47% of Germany's industrial growth, so impressive at the time to the many outside commentators unable to examine the detail, was directly accounted for by the rapid increase in military spending.

None of this should imply that there were no budgetary constraints on the development of tanks. There were, and they remained in place until the eve of the invasion of Poland, as we shall see. In the 1920s the money used to develop new weapons which were on the Versailles Treaty's banned list had to be concealed not only from the victors but in many cases from members of the government. When Hitler came to power, the more conservative elements within his government tried to restrain military spending, arguing that exports were required to bring foreign currency into the country and that consumers within Germany would demand a higher standard of living. In

1933 the Finance Ministry plan was for Germany to spend 35 billion Reichsmarks (RM) on rearmament spread over eight years, or about RM 4.3 billion per year.[12] Once Britain and France started to rearm, Germany poured more and more money into its own programmes in an effort to stay ahead and the 1933 allocations were clearly woefully insufficient.

Less than a year after the Nazis came to power, the Wehrmacht was already double the size allowed by Versailles, at 21 divisions. Two years later, in December 1935, Germany was planning on creating an army of 36 divisions; this in effect marked the switch from the defensive first phase into phase two, genuine preparations for wars of aggression, in which the tank was seen as the only weapon which could survive attacks on heavily fortified defences. The army of 36 divisions was to be made up of 12 corps each of three divisions: nine of these corps were entirely infantry but three of them were panzer corps, and these had one panzer division plus two infantry divisions. The 36-division plan was still sometimes referred to as the 'peacetime' army, because it was still thought by many senior generals to be too small: a genuine wartime

12 The exchange rate in 1933 was around RM 3.28 to the US dollar; for the rest of the 1930s it was around 2.5.

army required no fewer than 69 divisions: 63 infantry, 3 cavalry and 3 panzer. This aspiration, while ambitious in terms of sheer size, clearly shows that the reactionary elements in the army were still active. This was not a blueprint for a Blitzkrieg force; rather it was a traditional army with tanks bolted on. It tells us that in 1936 the panzer was still not thought of by everyone as the most important land weapon; this would not happen until after it had proved its point in 1939 and 1940.

Notwithstanding all this, the sudden expansion threw the rearmament budget out of the window; if the army was to expand as quickly as was being ordered by Berlin, the financial limits imposed upon it in 1933 would act as a brake. Therefore on 18 November 1936 the Defence Minister ordered the Wehrmacht simply to ignore the budgetary constraints imposed upon them by the Treasury in 1933. In the three years between 1937 and 1940, the army alone spent an average of RM 9 billion per annum, more than twice the original allocation for the entire armed forces. Hitler agreed with this strategy: he was not interested in exports, kitchen appliances, or financial orthodoxy; he wanted weapons, and was prepared both to squeeze the companies to produce them and to print money to pay for them.[13] After all, Germany was still, on the face of it, a capitalist economy and the contracts needed to be paid for.

On 15 October 1935 the 1st Panzer Division was formed at Weimar under General von Weichs, consisting of two regiments, each of two *Abteilungen* (battalions). In May 1936 the planned size of the army was increased again, to 43 divisions: three panzer divisions (plus four of motorised infantry) appeared on the order of battle. Each panzer division would require hundreds of tanks. Additionally, by 1939 seven independent panzer brigades were to have been created, each designed to allow expansion into a full division when ordered. And only one month later in June 1936 the shackles really came off – by October 1940 Germany was to be able to field a 102-division army of 3.6 million men.

Germany therefore needed to design,

13 In November 1939 he stated that 'One cannot win the war against England with cookers and washing-machines.'

RIGHT General Maximillian von Weichs was a cavalryman who was selected to command the Wehrmacht's first panzer division in 1935.

develop and produce many thousands of tanks to equip these new units. But the only tanks then in existence were the light Panzers I and II models, which even then were known to be inadequate in a war with a first-class power. What was needed were larger, more capable tanks, similar in size and capability to the *Grosstraktor* designs trialled by the Reichswehr. Two new, heavier tanks were to be introduced: the PzKpw III and the IV. Some 1,812 of these would be required for the new formations then planned, with one estimate suggesting that 870 of them should have been completed by the end of 1939. In fact, by 1 September 1939 only just over 300 of the new tanks had been completed, a clear indication that German tank production was failing miserably to meet demand.

This failure is a critical part of the story, not only of the Panzer III but more generally. Histories of the war frequently assume or imply that Germany went all out in the race to build the largest and most modern tank fleet in the world, with which it steamrollered through Poland, the Low Countries and France. The problem is that this simply was not so. German tank manufacture in the 1930s concentrated on the production of the Panzer Is and IIs to such an extent that at the start of the campaign against Poland, only 98 Panzer IIIs and 211 Panzer IVs had been built, compared with 1,445 Panzer Is and 1,223 Panzer IIs in service. Another way of looking at this is to

consider German tank production in terms of the percentage of the budget that was made available for it. Of the RM 35.6 billion spent on weapons between 1937 and 1941, artillery, guns and their ammunition took up nearly a third of the total at 32%. Static fortification measures claimed nearly 9%, whereas tanks, *including all other motor vehicles*, only received 4.7% of the total. Therefore it cannot be claimed that German tank design and manufacture was the priority, at least not until four years into the war – and by which time the Panzer III was about to be phased out of production.

Limitations on tank building were caused by three things: a lack of priority and urgency given to tanks; competition within the German industrial base for scarce manpower and machinery; and a lack of raw materials. Krupp was the fourth largest corporation in Germany, and it owned the enormous Gruson works near Magdeburg in Saxony, which produced the majority of the armour plate for Germany's rearmament programme and which was later to build many Panzer III turrets. However, the panzers were not the only weapons needing armour plate; the expanding navy and the extensive fortifications on both western and eastern frontiers required huge amounts, and these took priority over the production of tanks during the 1930s. The key point is that of priority. Had the panzers been given Hitler's full backing and allocated the pole position, they would have

ABOVE It's not all about numbers – but the hundred or so Panzer Is on parade here make for an impressive sight. *(TM 2587/E3)*

been built in much larger numbers. But they were not; Hitler initially gave the highest priority to the expansion of the Luftwaffe (and which throughout the war absorbed about 40% of the overall productive capacity of the state). He was also concerned about enemies attacking both Germany's western and/or eastern borders, and as a consequence large static fortifications were constructed. These required not only concrete but also steel – the larger plates used to protect gun emplacements could weigh as much as 38 tons each, the equivalent of nearly eight Panzer III tanks.[14] And the expansion of the Kriegsmarine was based upon large capital ships, requiring enormous quantities of steel and other scarce metals – even when concentrating on the construction of U-boats, the navy used up around 15% of the available production resources. As early as 1937 the state had to organise the collection of scrap and surplus metals from the population, which took in everything from municipal iron railings to spare keys and unused cutlery. In total, the two main beneficiaries of productive capability were aircraft and ammunition production, which used up between 65 and 70% of the available resources.

The speed of the rearmament expansion also caused problems to the extent that steel rationing was introduced as early as 23 February 1937, and thereafter all amendments to allocations had to be personally approved by Hitler using the mechanism of the Führer Principle or *Führerprizip*. This particularly affected the army, and the ration of steel they received was insufficient to build the weapons they had planned for, especially tanks. By September 1937 the army was only receiving 30% of the steel it needed for its new weapons programmes. Hitler did not approve an increase in the steel ration for the army until June 1938, and by August over a third of German steel production was allocated for the army … but this only lasted until the following spring, when swingeing cuts were made once again to the army's ration. Of course, this toing and froing did not constrain the recruitment of the infantry soldiers who required less sophisticated equipment and which was continued, but it

condemned the majority of the German army to dependency on two forms of transport: jackbooted feet and horses' hooves. Owing to these limitations it was estimated that the German army could not be at the desired 1940 order of battle until spring 1943.

This situation was exacerbated by the acceleration towards war. Once Hitler was confident that the defensive phase was complete, by 1936 he had begun to set targets for the armed forces to work towards, initially on the assumption that war would not be required until 1943. However, his 1935 declaration that Germany was rearming had caused the other states, particularly France and Britain, to reluctantly accelerate their own rearmament, and this triggered an arms race. Hitler therefore had to calculate when Germany was at its optimum strength compared with its potential enemies, and at that point, there was nothing to be gained by waiting. In late September 1938, orders were secretly issued to German generals to prepare for war – with Britain – in 1942. At least partly in response to this, on 14 October Goering announced that the existing rearmament programme was to be enlarged and speeded up, and the army was to procure large quantities of offensive weapons, including 'heavy tanks'. 'Heavy' in this context clearly meant the heaviest at that time, the Panzers III and IV. Unfortunately for the army, priorities again came into play and now it was time for the Kriegsmarine to be given precedence by Hitler, the decision being announced on 27 January 1939. Further steel rationing followed and, in July 1939, the tank production programme – which had not had time to reap the benefits of the short-term increase agreed in June 1938 – was cut in half. The programme had aimed to construct 1,200 medium tanks (Panzer IIIs and IVs) between October 1939 and October 1940, a rate of 100 per month. With the forced movement of workers from tank production into other industries, any future rapid expansion of tank production would be all but impossible, and so it proved. Because of the expansion throughout Germany, skilled workers could expect to find full employment: average unemployment in 1933 had been 4.8 million. By 1938 it was down to only 429,000, and those left unemployed were the least useful and

14 The actual amount of armour used on the Panzer III – as opposed to the all-up weight – was about a third of the total: this was about 5 tons (early models) increasing to more than 6 tons on later tanks.

lowest-skilled workers. This, plus the increasing conscription into the Wehrmacht, served to handicap the tank-building companies when they were asked (told) to increase production in the years to come. How much the lack of skilled workers impacted upon the quality of the finished product is hard to assess, but quantity was certainly affected.

As Germany was still functioning – at least on the surface – as a capitalist economy with companies which required payment for their productive efforts, how was this managed? Each Panzer III cost approximately RM 100,000 after all. The answer was by sleight of hand and outright coercion, within a framework that the Nazis devised called the *wehrwirtschaft*, or defence economy. This new extreme method of doing business followed no conventional economic model; indeed, Hitler himself seemed to believe that economics could be entirely controlled by policy, and said that his system was 'subject to different internal laws'. If they were laws, they were laws of his own design. On 20 March 1939 the New Finance Plan imposed a new method of business upon the Wehrmacht's suppliers. Rather than being paid wholly in cash, they were forced to accept at least 40% of the contract price in the form of tax credits, which attracted no interest and could only be redeemed in the (unspecified) future. It amounted to a forced loan, but by this stage, Hitler was all-powerful and complaining was not only fruitless but potentially dangerous. Given this state of affairs, Germany was committed to going to war before its economy collapsed. The die, forged over the preceding years, was now cast.

German doctrine and the need for two medium tanks

In the midst of the ever-changing plans and diktats coming from Berlin, the staff within the newly formed *Panzerwaffe* (the armoured force) had to develop the vehicles that allowed them to train, and then to fight. The actual tanks to be used would be designed from scratch, to meet specifications known as *Technische Lieferbedingungen* (technical delivery terms) that were based upon their perceived roles; in other words, the weapons were to be specifically built to match the doctrine. The first two tanks

LEFT Heinz Guderian was possibly the most celebrated German tank general, whose understanding of armour surpassed that of Rommel; Liddell-Hart called him 'a single-minded soldier'. As a lieutenant colonel in 1931 he had been appointed as Chief of Staff to the newly created Inspectorate of Motor Troops.

built under the Nazi regime, the Panzers I and II, were too small and light to be useful in a full-scale war; the rising star of the *Panzerwaffe* General Guderian stated plainly that they were to be regarded as training vehicles and unsuitable for combat. What the Germans required were heavier tanks that would be decisive on the battlefield.

Although later in the war the Germans tended to develop heavier and heavier tanks, searching for armour immunity and unstoppable firepower, in the mid-1930s their aspirations were much more realistic. In the quest to produce weapons to suit the doctrine, the Wehrmacht decided to introduce two varieties of medium tank, each with a distinct role. The first was to become the Panzer III: this was to be the primary equipment of the panzer divisions, and was to be extremely mobile in order to make breakthrough and breakout of enemy defensive positions a reality. Additionally – and here is the crucial difference with other nations' doctrines – it was to be armed with a weapon meant primarily for destroying enemy tanks. Whereas other countries tried to convince themselves that tanks would not fight other tanks, Germany recognised that situation as the natural state of affairs on a modern battlefield, and thus armed itself with a tank that was optimised for that role. The other tank was the Panzer IV, initially codenamed

be built with a larger 64in turret ring. It was this characteristic that later allowed the Panzer IV to accept a more powerful gun and thus take over the role of battle tank from the Panzer III, as we shall see.

Design and development of the Panzer III

In late 1934, development contracts were issued to four companies, following the normal practice. The firms were: Daimler, Krupp, MAN and Rheinmetall, with the latter given the task of designing the turret which would be common to all the prototypes. (Rheinmetall's chief turret designer was a certain Herr Zimmer, who seems to have designed the turrets for both Panzers III and IV, hence the similarities.) It will be recalled that with the exception of MAN, these were the companies which had been involved in the design of the *Grosstraktor* in the 1920s, and were therefore the ones best suited to the complexity of the task. When the orders went out, it was still thought necessary to give such projects cover names to disguise what they were: in this case, the name used was *Zugführerwagen* (ZW), or platoon commander's vehicle.[17] (Apparently German industry continued to refer to tanks by their original codenames right through until the end of the war. A senior Henschel engineer under interrogation in 1945 at their experimental establishment in Haustenbeck always referred to the Panzer III as the ZW.)

The ZW – we shall call it the Panzer III from this point – was specified to weigh no more than 15 tons; this was in order to keep the power-to-weight ratio up and ensure manoeuvrability, as well as in recognition that the eventual weight of the tank in service was likely to exceed this. Standard German philosophy at this stage was that a tank should have its maximum armour over the frontal aspect (*ie* what one could see if standing directly in front of it), and this area should be immune to one's own weapon. For the Panzer III the desired solution was for it to be able to withstand the French 25mm Hotchkiss gun firing at 100m, not a particularly good choice of threat weapon as it turned out,

ABOVE The Krupp-designed MKA, a rejected contender for the Panzer III contract, but which displayed many features that were adopted on the Panzer IV.

BELOW A wooden mock-up of the Panzer III. Note the rounded front hull but especially the hatched marks instructing the carpenters to shave off the front turret corners, a typical design feature and one which may be ascribed to the turret designer, Herr Zimmer. *(Tank Museum)*

Begleitwagen (BW), meaning support vehicle.[15] Although still classed as a medium tank, it was heavier than the Panzer III, with a target weight of 20 tons, a third heavier than its lookalike cousin. Its purpose was to support the Panzer III by delivering high-explosive shells against targets other than enemy tanks; it was not, crucially, an infantry support tank as envisaged by both the French and British armies; rather, at this stage it was closer to being a self-propelled gun, albeit one with many of the attributes of a tank (more armour, revolving turret) and designed purely to support the battle tanks.[16] Although both tanks, not surprisingly, ended up heavier than the original weight specified, the Panzer IV was slightly bigger in all respects, and critically was 500mm (19in) wider, allowing it to

15 For many years it was thought to mean *Battalionwagen*, but most commentators now think this to be erroneous. However, German tank engineers used the term *Battalionwagen* when under interrogation in 1945 and it is more consistent with the ZW codename given to the Panzer III.
16 Infantry support tanks were extremely heavily armoured, slow-moving and allocated to infantry formations for which they worked.

17 It was also sometimes referred to as: *Versuchtkraftfahrzeug* 619 (VK, or experimental vehicle); *Mittlerer Traktor* (Medium Tractor); and/or 3.7cm *Geschutz Panzerwagen* (3.7cm gun tank).

as it was less effective than the German 37mm. Less armour would have to be carried on the sides, and less still at the rear, in order to keep the overall weight down, but this was accepted as a necessary evil. Another weight-limiting factor at the design stage was the carrying capacity of typical German bridges. However, like the majority of tanks, over its life it became heavier, as weapon sizes were increased and more (and more) armour was found to be necessary. This led to more powerful engines being required, which although adding more power could come with the penalty of yet more weight. The requirement for more stowage and especially additional fuel (and water) also became clear once it had been used in combat, and so the tank in its final form weighed over 50% more than the planned 15 tons. But that was in the future.

In terms of armour protection it was less than impressive. At 30mm frontal (and only 10mm in places) by 1940 its armour would only have been classed as moderate at best, being overmatched by both types of British infantry tank as well as the French Char B and S35, among others.[18] However, its 250hp petrol engine would give it a power-to-weight ratio of around 13:1, making it much more manoeuvrable on the battlefield than those tanks. Additionally, it had the advantages of a very roomy three-man turret with a commander's cupola and the efficiency that this provided, and all tanks were equipped with radio receivers as a minimum. The key design feature of the Panzer III as originally conceived was for it to mount a high-velocity 50mm anti-tank gun … which had yet to be designed. Development work on the gun only started in January 1938 at Rheinmetall and had it been prioritised, it would have been the most potent weapon available in 1940, outclassing both the British 2-pounder (40mm) and the French 47mm. As we shall discover, a 50mm gun was only finally fitted on to the tank in the second half of 1940, and it started life with a much smaller gun. With its original specification it had promised to be a genuine battle-winner, but its potential was marred by a sensible military decision.

Standardisation is something that all armies strive for but few achieve, despite

18 By 1944 the Tiger tank was mounting 40mm of armour on the turret roof.

ABOVE The Panzer III was designed with German bridge capacity in mind, but did not take into account the much weaker wooden bridges that would be encountered in Russia. *(Bundesarchiv)*

BELOW The Somua S35 – heavy cast armour and a 47mm gun made it formidable on paper, but the one-man turret and lack of radios made it less than efficient as a combat tank.

understanding the production and logistic benefits that it brings. The Wehrmacht was very poor at achieving standardisation in most areas, operating a bewildering variety of incompatible vehicles from a range of manufacturers who did not co-operate with one another. But the army was adamant that weapon, and particularly ammunition, standardisation was to be achieved, and decreed that certain calibres were to be adopted as the standard. In the mid-1930s 50mm was not one of those calibres, as it was too small for use by field artillery but thought to be too large for infantry-manned anti-tank guns; adopting it solely for tank use was not viewed as beneficial, and so the Panzer III specification was altered so that it was to use a version of the 37mm PaK gun recently adopted by the infantry. Despite the protestations of the Panzer generals the decision was made, and the 37mm was adopted. Fortunately – and it was fortune and not clever design – the vehicle itself was in too far advanced a state of design to consider making major changes, so the hull width and large turret ring were retained, and which, although unnecessarily large for the 37mm gun, would prove to be so important by the end of 1940.

A very good question which we briefly considered earlier is why Germany bothered to design, develop and field two tanks that looked and weighed much the same, rather than concentrating on selecting the best design and making two versions that differed only in the guns carried. There are a number of interrelated answers to this question that are worth exploring. Firstly, there is the matter of doctrine. Germany saw the Panzer III and IV in different terms, as the former was to be a highly mobile exploitation tank, designed to wreak havoc in rear areas using armour-piercing ammunition and machine-gun fire (hence the early models all having dual machine guns in the turret), whereas the Panzer IV was simply a support weapon for the Panzer III, able to neutralise anti-tank guns and engage targets at longer ranges using high-explosive shells, and fitted with a single turret machine gun. As a support tank it did not need to be as manoeuvrable as its lighter cousin, and thus the Panzer IV could carry slightly more armour and end up as the heavier tank of the two. Because of the philosophy of commissioning a number of firms to produce early concept models of a new tank and then selecting the preferred model for full development, it was unlikely that the same company would win both competitions, and so the tanks developed would have many common features but would differ significantly in detailed design. This tendency was reinforced by the military oversight of each design, whereby the companies did not have a completely free hand but were closely supervised and guided during the design process. When selecting the winning model, the authorities were always prepared to cut across normal commercial practice and incorporate good ideas from other manufacturers

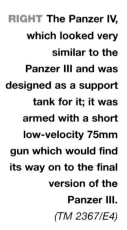

RIGHT The Panzer IV, which looked very similar to the Panzer III and was designed as a support tank for it; it was armed with a short low-velocity 75mm gun which would find its way on to the final version of the Panzer III. (TM 2367/E4)

RIGHT The sections of the hull tub, with the 11 plates of the Panzer III (top) and the larger but simpler eight-part Panzer IV (below).

CENTRE A comparison of the superstructures on the Panzer III (top) and Panzer IV (below), with the all-important hull width and thus turret ring sizes shown. Note that the Panzer III did not feature access hatches for the two crewmen in the hull. The blue component is the *bugpanzer*, which was thicker as it protected the driver, radio operator, and the fighting compartment. The rear *heckpanzer* (green) covered the engine compartment. Although both parts were of welded construction, they were then bolted together and on to the hull to allow maintenance and repair.

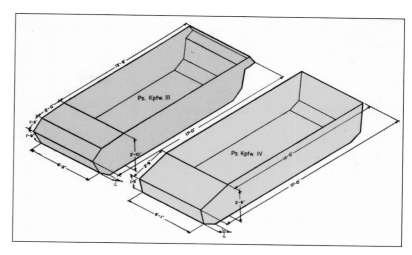

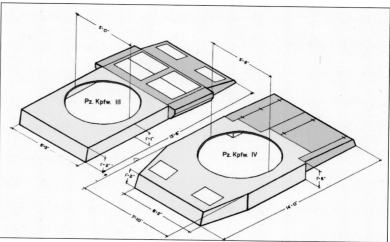

into the chosen design, as well as insisting on certain common components that must be used. This led to a situation whereby both tank turrets were designed by the same company (Rheinmetall – and so probably by the same chief designer, Herr Zimmer), and both used the same Maybach engine. Although the hull designs looked outwardly similar, they were constructed in very different ways, and the Panzer IV design was easier to build as it used fewer plates and therefore less materials and welding time. This advantage would not become immediately apparent, but by 1942 such production advantages were recognised as very important.

One of the key differences between the two tanks was that the IV did not use a torsion bar suspension system but relied on semi-elliptical leaf springs, a system that could not be made to work on the Panzer III, as we shall discover. The probable reason for this was that Krupp, the design parent for the Panzer IV, had a strong background in making railway engines and rolling stock and understood how to make a 'paired roadwheel longitudinal leaf-spring suspension' operate on a tank chassis, whereas Daimler, responsible for the Panzer III, was in essence a road vehicle company and tended to prefer technology from that area. Additionally, the Panzer IV did not need to be as manoeuvrable as the Panzer III as its tactical role was different, and so the use of the technically elegant but compromised torsion bar system

BELOW The *heckpanzer* unbolted as a separate component. This is a later version with the original flat hatches replaced by the mushroom air inlets introduced to improve engine cooling in North Africa. *(TM 6316/B2)*

RIGHT The main production (red) and training (blue) locations referred to in this book, shown on a map of modern-day Germany. The Breslau factory is now in Poland (Wroclaw).

was not thought to be necessary. Despite the many differences, both tanks did in fact enjoy a large amount of commonality, including at times the same basic models of engine and gearbox. Even though the suspensions were very different, the tracks were of the same design. As already noted, the majority of the companies that built the tanks simply acted as assemblers, and many of the component parts were brought in from elsewhere. Therefore companies like Bosch, Siemens, Notek, Telefunken, etc., all supplied the same parts to both tanks. British examination revealed that radios and communications equipment, weapons, hatches, visors, telescopes and periscopes were all interchangeable to a large degree (bearing in mind the various models of both tanks all had their differences). However, this was no different to British practice, and can only be considered as partial standardisation at best, as it certainly helped the war effort but crucially did not enable the Germans to produce more tanks when needed.

The Panzer III had a crew of five. In addition to the three men in the turret – commander, gunner and loader – two were mounted in the hull. The driver was in the front left and the radio operator, who also manned the bow machine gun, in the front right. All three of the development companies were closely monitored so that their hull designs were in many respects similar, the intention being that they would all meet the specification, but were instructed to utilise certain characteristics in each design so that the pros and cons could be quickly recognised. The prototypes were extensively

tested on the Kummersdorf and Münsingen training areas starting in late 1936, with the Daimler design being selected in early 1937, although some features from the others were retained. A British report later identified the main hull designer as Otto Merker, who had worked in Sweden, but this has not been confirmed.

In most ways the basic design was sound, and although it eventually ran to 12 main models with a number of other variants, the biggest difficulty initially was found in getting the suspension right. Four different types were tried on the *Ausfuhrung* (models) A to D, before finally settling on the configuration of six roadwheel pairs each side with torsion bar suspension adopted on the Ausf E. An important point to note was that – like many other tanks – the Panzer III was designed mainly for the conditions in which it was believed that it was to operate – central Europe. This led to difficulties being encountered when it had to fight in other, extreme conditions, notably the severe winters in Russia and the heat and dust of the North African desert.[19] It was not officially accepted into service until 27 September 1939, nearly a month after it made its combat debut in Poland. In general terms we can group the evolution of the tank into the following categories:

■ Ausf A–D	Development models with different suspension configurations
■ Ausf E–F (early)	Battle tank with 37mm L/45 gun
■ Ausf F (late)–J	Battle tank with 50mm L/42 gun
■ Ausf L–M	Battle tank with 50mm L/60 gun
■ Ausf N	Support tank with 75mm L/24 gun

'Ausf' is short for *Ausfuhrung*, literally meaning execution. There is nothing sinister in this, a less literal but more usable translation is model, in the sense of a design project ending up as a model produced as the result. Another non-literal translation that can be

19 Russian summers also delivered a lot of heat and dust with similar effects on machinery and men, and North Africa could be bitterly cold at night.

used is batch. Although it is common now for people interested in the topic to become quite excited – this is an understatement – about the identifying features of each Ausf, at the time the majority of the Wehrmacht, including the crews, couldn't care less: they tended to refer to either the Panzer III 3.7cm or the Panzer III 5.0cm. With the latter, after the introduction of the L/60 gun they sometimes added *kurz* (short) or *lang* (long) to clarify. The personnel who did care about which Ausf was which were the logistic and maintenance personnel, as they needed to order the correct spare parts to carry out repairs. And a word of caution is appropriate here. Because many older models were rearmed, up-armoured and otherwise modified, as the war progressed it became increasingly common to see tanks that displayed features of two Ausfs, making exact identification of their former or indeed current model difficult. And occasionally, just to muddy the waters further, the designations could change when it was felt that a major modification meant that the newer designation was more appropriate than the old. In this way, tanks ordered as Ausf J (with the L/42 gun) but fitted during production with the L/60 gun were referred to as Ausf L, the new designation being introduced at the end of March 1942.

The *Sonderkraftfahrzeug* (SdKfz) designation was another method of classification. It was devised for army ordnance purposes and given to vehicles as a means of differentiating them, but it did not specify the same level of detail as the Ausf system. Therefore, identifying a vehicle as SdKfz 141 could mean anything from an Ausf A to J. The SdKfz designations used on the Panzer III series were:

- SdKfz 141   Ausf A–J
- SdKfz 141/1   Ausf L and M
- SdKfz 141/2   Ausf N
- SdKfz 141/3   *Flammpanzer* III
- SdKfz 143   *Artillerie Panzerbeobach-tungswagen* III
- SdKfz 266   *PanzerBefehlsWagen* III
- SdKfz 267   *PanzerBefehlsWagen* III
- SdKfz 268   *PanzerBefehlsWagen* III

We will investigate these specialist tanks and variants in Chapter 2.

Forming and expanding the Panzer units

Because of the need for secrecy, Germany did not form any dedicated tank units until after Hitler came to power. Although training and experiments were carried out by the Reichswehr, no operational units were ever formed. The first true tank unit came into being on 1 November 1933, and bore the somewhat lengthy title *Kraftfahrlehrkommando Zossen*, meaning 'motorised training command at Zossen', south of Berlin. In 1933 there was still the need to use a disguised name for the benefit of the outside world, but it was a real combat unit, although resources were limited. Only four of the *Grosstraktor*, four of the *Leichttraktor* plus six training chassis known as *Kleintraktor* were available at first. The 1st Training Company, not surprisingly, included a number of personnel who had trained at Kama. Very quickly it expanded into battalion strength, and by 1 November 1934 was a full regiment with two battalions. Just prior to that, on 12 October, the organisation chart for a proposed panzer division was published, and this was trialled on exercises in August the following year. Actual tanks remained a scarce resource: in March 1935 the two battalions only possessed 12 real tanks between them. Weak and immature, nevertheless the Germans had their first panzer division. On 1 September 1934 orders were given that the 2nd Pz Div was to be formed by 1 October 1935, and in the spirit of the rapid expansion taking place

BELOW One of the very first Panzer IIIs: an Ausf A in Berlin. This is probably the parade ordered by Hitler on 26 September 1938 as part of his psychological warfare during the Sudeten crisis. Note the complicated and vulnerable exhaust system on the hull rear.

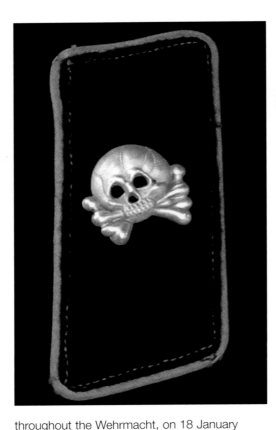

RIGHT The *Totenkopf* or death's-head insignia – nothing to do with the SS – and rose pink *waffenfarbe* of the *Panzerwaffe*; the colour had been used by the motor transport troops of the Reichswehr. The 24th Panzer Division uniquely used golden yellow, the traditional cavalry colour, instead of pink.

BELOW An illustration from a Maybach brochure, showing how the engine (here marked as 300hp) fitted in the rear, with the transmission in the front, leaving a large area for the fighting compartment between the two.

throughout the Wehrmacht, on 18 January 1935 it was decreed that three panzer divisions and three independent panzer brigades were to be in existence by 1 October 1935. These brigades were to be structured to allow future expansion into a full division at a later stage. On 15 October 1935 the need for secrecy was deemed to be a thing of the past, and the cover names were dropped; in future, the names would announce what they were.

Early development models: Ausf A–D

All of the first 100 tanks – 70 gun-armed and 30 command – were built by Daimler-Benz at the Marienfelde plant in south Berlin. The Ausf

TABLE 1: PRODUCTION AUSF A–D

AUSF	FAHRGESTELL (CHASSIS NUMBER)	NUMBER
A	60101–60110	10
B	60201–60215	15
C	60301–60315	15
D	60221–60225 60316–60340	30
Befehls D[1]	60341–60370	30

A was the first to arrive, with ten being built starting in late 1936 but which were not ready to be delivered for trials until the second half of 1937.[20] The first four models all used the same engine – a Maybach HL108 TR petrol unit. This was a V12 dry sump engine, which produced a healthy 250hp at 2,800rpm. Ausf A–C all used a ZF five-speed and reverse SFG75 or SSG75 gearbox, and used two fuel tanks, each holding 150 litres, sufficient for a range of 165km on roads. At the rear of the hull, the exhaust silencer was mounted externally. The design of the turret was by Rheinmetall, which experimented with slightly different configurations and probably for reasons of speed and convenience used riveting and bolting, whereas later turrets would be of welded construction. An internal mantlet was used for mounting the main armament, which was the 37mm L/45 KwK 36 gun derived from the PaK 36 anti-tank gun. Some 121 rounds of ammunition could be carried. Alongside it on the right were two MG34 machine guns, slightly offset from each other to allow double drum magazines to be used. The MGs were mounted on their own trunnions allowing them to be elevated or depressed independently of the 37mm. The intention here seems to have been that it allowed the loader to operate the MGs independently of the gunner – the loader had his own traverse handle in his side of the turret. A rudimentary drum cupola was fitted to the rear of the turret and a number of vision flaps (visors) were fitted around the tank for the crew to use. As the tank was a development model, it was made with very thin armour: a maximum

20 Five went to Wunstorf, one to the gunnery school at Putlos and two each to Panzer Regiments 1 and 5.

ABOVE An Ausf A in a two-colour grey and brown camouflage scheme. Note the two square bolted access hatches on the nose, deleted on production tanks, and the horn in the centre of the vertical plate. *(Tank Museum)*

BELOW This Ausf A shows how the radio antenna was initially mounted, where it could be raised and lowered by the radio operator in the hull. The trough appears to be made of metal, whereas on service tanks wood was used.

TOP AND ABOVE Early turret designs. This is the type used on vehicles 1 to 10 (Ausf A). Note the design of the 'dustbin' cupola, the square rear pistol ports and the single-piece side doors.

ABOVE The twin MG34 mounting used on the early tanks with the 37mm gun; the *doppeltrommel* drum-fed MGs were mounted on their own trunnions, which could be unlocked, thus allowing elevation independent of the main armament. This is possibly a developmental mounting, as the butts were not often used on service tanks.

RIGHT A German postcard showing an Ausf A on trials (or training), probably in 1937. This sort of thing was only possible once the Nazis had abandoned the veil of secrecy surrounding the development of their armoured forces.

Unfer Heer
Panzertruppen: Kampfwagen

LEFT The cone on the turret roof concealed a circular port for signals flags, although why it was felt necessary to disguise it is unclear; it was deleted during Ausf E and F production. The nose access hatches are now hinged and circular, a distinctive feature of the Ausf B. *(Tank Museum)*

of 14.5mm on the hull was no greater than that carried on the Panzer I, although 16mm was used on the turret front, but the belly plate was a paper-thin 5mm. A FuG 5 transmitter/receiver or a FuG 2 receiver were fitted as standard.

The most important difference between the four development models was the suspension. Ausf A had a system of five pairs of largish rubber-tyred roadwheels each side, with a vertical coil spring on each station for shock absorption. Two top roller track support wheels were fitted above and slightly forward of wheels three and five. The tracks were 360mm wide, with 96 links per side. This suspension was found to be unsatisfactory and so Ausf B switched to eight pairs of small roadwheels per side, this time using horizontal leaf springs: these were arranged in a 4–4 configuration so that the front and rear groups of four wheels were each mounted together on a bracket, with a leaf spring and shock absorber above. A third top roller was introduced, above the gap between wheels one and two. Aside from a slightly different style of cupola, the tank was otherwise much the same as the Ausf A, although trench-crossing and vertical step-

ABOVE AND RIGHT The second turret type, with a different cupola design but still employing more bolts and rivets than would be used on the service tank. A muzzle cover is fitted to the 37mm.

RIGHT Five of the Ausf B chassis were used to develop the prototype Sturmgeschutz III around 1938: this is one of the five. *(Tank Museum)*

LEFT Ausf C: the square nose hatches have returned, and the maximum armour thickness has been doubled to 30mm. This was the last model to use the one-piece turret side doors. *(Tank Museum)*

climbing were both modestly improved. Fifteen Ausf Bs were produced during 1937. The same number of Ausf Cs were also made, between June 1937 and January 1938, and merely tinkered with the suspension used on Ausf B, with the small wheels now grouped into a 2–4–2 configuration. The front and rear pair had their own leaf spring and shock absorber, while the centre four shared a common leaf spring but no shock absorber was provided. One post-war report indicated that the suspension on the Ausf A had been designed by Daimler, whereas the leaf spring types used on the Ausf B–D came from the MAN design team – an example of how the best features from different companies could be utilised.

Ausf D was the final attempt to get the eight roadwheel suspension right, with 30 built over an 18-month period starting in January 1938. The front and rear leaf springs were now set at a slight angle, and the shock absorbers had to be relocated as a result; the front top roller was also moved slightly further back from the sprocket. New sprockets and idler designs were introduced. An improved design of cast cupola was fitted and, significantly, the armour basis was much improved, up to a maximum of 30mm – which of course added considerable weight. While the engine remained largely unchanged, mechanical fuel pumps replaced the previous electric models, the cooling system was modified, and the engine decks redesigned. The Ausf D used a ZF six-speed SSG76 unit, and the same amount of fuel was carried, but in four 75-litre armoured tanks.

ABOVE A partially completed Ausf D hull ready for a test drive before the turret is fitted, with a hood fitted above the driver's front plate. *(Tank Museum)*

BELOW An Ausf D¹ command tank in the snows of Russia – literally. It appears to mount the earlier Ausf C cupola. Note the amount of track links on the hull front, under the snow.

Chapter Two

Service tanks and variants

───(●)────────

The Panzer III ran to eight main models, known as *Ausfuhrung*. Three different guns were used, along with increasing amounts of armour. As the war progressed and Germany's situation worsened, attempts were made to improve the tank while making it easier to manufacture, which took the tank as far as it could. Identifying the different models is key to understanding the varying capabilities that each brought to the battlefield.

OPPOSITE Britain captured a number of different models of the Panzer III in North Africa from 1941 onwards and subjected them to detailed examination. Many features of the tanks were found to be novel and advanced, although a few design or production flaws were also recorded.

Production

On 1 January 1940, after the completion of the Polish campaign and before the attacks on Denmark and Norway in April, the reported strengths in each panzer division operating the Panzer III was as follows: 1st Pz Div – 38; 2nd Pz Div – 13; 3rd Pz Div – 12; 4th Pz Div – 12; 5th Pz Div – 13. This meant that only 88 Panzer IIIs were in the hands of the field army, which was 36% of the tanks produced up to that date. It can be readily appreciated from this that production was much too slow to equip the divisions with the new battle tank at the rate required. This led to the continuing necessity to rely upon other types to fill the gaps, meaning the lighter and less capable Czech 38(t), and the even lighter and even less capable 35(t), with nearly 300 in service making up (part of) the shortfall. In the summer of 1940 Fritz Todt, responsible for weapons production, set up a special committee (*SonderausschussesPanzerwagen*) to make tank production more efficient, under the stewardship of Walther 'Panzer' Rohland of the Deutsche Edelstahlwerke.

Despite production commencing as early as 1937, the peak production months for the Panzer III were not to be reached until April and May 1942, when 246 were built in each of those months.[1] This was roughly comparable with British monthly production of a similar type, the Crusader, but that was not the point; by then US and (especially) Soviet production was going into overdrive. Hitler was later quoted as saying: 'I, the head of the greatest industrial nation, assisted by the greatest genius of all time [meaning Speer] sweat and toil to produce just six hundred tanks a month, and you are telling me that Stalin makes a thousand!' And by 1941 the USA (as yet not at war with anyone) was producing almost as many armaments as Britain or Germany, demonstrating its huge potential as 'the arsenal of democracy'. It is noteworthy that American-style assembly-line techniques were not employed by the German tank-building firms, each tank being built at a station rather than being passed along a constantly moving belt. Production always lagged behind the needs of the troops – in July 1941 losses of German tanks were 275% of monthly production, and often hovered perilously close to or even above the 100% mark.[2] As late as July 1941 the Germans, planning on raising a total of 36 panzer divisions, were still reckoning on the Panzer III being the main battle tank, with 7,992 being needed. However, by November 1941 the army had realised that the Panzer III, even when rearmed with the long L/60 gun, was going to be no match for the T34 and the tank was therefore obsolescent. Despite this, the following year saw Panzer III production rise by about 50% to reach its peak; in other words, the organisation knowingly produced tanks that were out of date, but could not throttle back their production until better designs started to become available.

BELOW A Panzer III and StuG III production factory. Note that this is *not* a modern assembly line, but rather all tanks are being constructed individually on a station which is set at 90° to the floor direction – an inefficient process.

---

1   The maximum for the Panzer IV was 334 in June 1944.
2   For example: September 1941 70%; October 1941 75%; November 1941 100%; December 1941 150%; January 1942 125%; February 1942 75%; July 1942 100%; and November 1942 125%. The worst month of the war was February 1943, when losses were 500% of that month's production. By comparison the Battle of Kursk (July 1943) was 125%.

TABLE 2A: GUN TANK PRODUCTION BY MONTH

	1939	1940		1941	1942		1943	
	37mm	37mm	50mm	50mm	50mm	75mm	50mm	75mm
January	2	42	0	88	159	0	46	0
February	2	49	0	108	216	0	22	12
March	0	51	0	92	244	0	0	35
April	2	51	0	124	246	0	0	46
May	4	65	0	143	246	0	0	43
June	8	58	0	133	228	0	0	11
July	11	67	17	127	139	92	0	0
August	20	3	84	179	90	141	0	20
September	40	5	86	178	75	142	0	0
October	40	5	95	164	116	72	0	0
November	35	0	82	206	178	0	0	0
December	42	0	102	171	221	0	0	0
Total by gun type	206	396	466	1,713	2,158	447	68	167
Total in year	206	862		1,713	2,605		235	
Monthly average	17	72		143	217		20	
Peak (best month)	42	102		206	246		46	

The famous automobile company Daimler-Benz fulfilled the role of what in Britain would be called the design parent, responsible for designing, developing and improving the hull and overall layout, with Rheinmetall taking the lead on turret and gun development; indeed, all tanks built up to and including the Ausf D were made by Daimler. From the Ausf E onwards a number of other companies were involved in constructing the Panzer III in order to increase production capability;[3] these firms were:

- Altmärkische Kettenwerk GmbH Berlin (Alkett)
- Fahrzeug und Motorenbau GmbH Breslau (FAMO)
- Henschel und Sohn AG Kassel[4]
- Maschinenfabrik Augsburg Nürnberg (MAN)
- Maschinenfabrik Niededesachsen-Hanover (MNH)
- Muhlenbau und Industrie AG Braunschweig (MIAG)[5]

Table 2B below shows how these construction firms joined – and in some cases left – the construction programme. Note that it is

3   This was not done, however, to reduce the risk of lost production should a factory be attacked from the air, as this threat was not thought to be credible at the time.

4   Wegmann (Kassel) were responsible for fitting the turrets to many of the Henschel-made hulls, which almost certainly made completion of these tanks a longer process than those made in a single plant.
5   In mid-1942 Henschel, Alkett and MIAG all stopped Panzer III production in order to produce Stug III.

TABLE 2B: TANK PRODUCTION BY MANUFACTURER

	Ausf A–D	Ausf E	Ausf F	Ausf G	Ausf H	Ausf J–N	Command	Flamethrower	Total
MIAG	0	0	0	80	72	1,126	0	100	1,378
Daimler-Benz	70	41	45*	60	50	699	300	0	1,265
Henschel	0	0	170*	155	66	716	81	0	1,188
MAN	0	55	96	90	98	724	0	0	1,063
MNH	0	0	0	50	0	743	0	0	793
Alkett	0	0	96	150	0	350	0	0	596
FAMO	0	0	28	15	0	0	0	0	43
Total	70	96	435	600	286	4,358	381	100	6,326

*Henschel completed 50 of the 95 Ausf F tanks contracted to D-B.

RIGHT The MNH plant
layout in Hanover; the
railway spur ran from
the west (left) along
the northern (top)
boundary of
the factory.

sometimes impossible to determine precisely which model was produced and these cases are labelled as Ausf J–N.

The use of the word 'constructing' in referring to the companies is deliberate; the main armoured components – hull, superstructure and turrets – were often made by other firms, for example DEW in Hanover, who between 1936 and 1942 produced 1,954 hull tubs, 1,867 hull superstructures, and 1,907 Panzer III turrets, but did not assemble a single tank. The main components were then shipped to the assemblers who also received smaller parts from any number of other firms (Rheinmetall, Maybach, ZF, Bosch, etc.) and built them up into finished tanks. Some companies did make some of the required components on site; for example MIAG had their own foundry for making tank tracks. (Even fairly straightforward items took a lot of time to produce if the design was less than simple and there was an insistence of the maintenance of quality: one set of tracks would take around 2,000 man hours to cast and finish.) It was noticed by British experts that many of the smaller components – cupola, hatches, visors, etc. – bore the company marks of several different steelworks. The assemblers had the job of putting them all together, and making them fit where necessary, using skilled workers for the task. This led to a lot of production time being wasted on hand finishing, and in some instances led to 'standardised' parts being modified for a particular tank, and not readily usable on another.

Examination of the site plans of a number of German tank production facilities reveals that they all had one thing in common: easy access to a railhead, generally on site. Because of the need to ship in hulls, turrets, guns, etc., plus a myriad of other smaller components from around Germany, it was essential that these could be moved straight into the plants with the minimum of trouble. Strange though it may seem, the tanks often left the plants fully kitted out, with the notable exception of radio items, but with a full complement of ammunition. The finished tanks could then be transported into the army ordnance depots for final preparation including the fitting of radio equipment and issued to troops; in the case of the Panzer III, issues never appear to have been made directly from the plants to troops. The access to railways therefore created a potential bottleneck in production that the Allies could have exploited more than they did – no railways, no tanks. This could apply equally to sub-components: Rheinmetall-Borsig made the 50mm KwK 38 gun in Düsseldorf, but the breech blocks for it were made in Bochum, 50km away. The Allied strategic bombing campaign concentrated on bombing civilian areas (RAF by night) or specific high-value factories (USAAF by day), and the bombing campaign does not seem to have affected Panzer III production to any great extent.

Each major component had its own serial number, and these did not always match, so

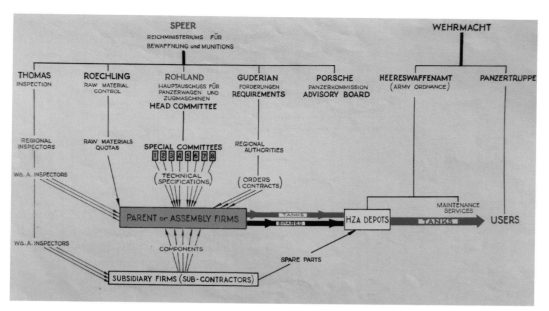

LEFT A post-war British report used this diagram to illustrate the German tank production system from about 1942 with Speer in charge of munitions and Rohland under him in control of tanks. The HZA Depots were the ordnance depots where radios, etc., were fitted.

that a vehicle might have a hull with a different number to the turret and superstructure. However, the whole vehicle was given an overall *Fahrgestellnummer* or chassis number, which was used for identification purposes in much the same way as a British registration or US serial number. These were painted in red block numerals inside the driver's compartment, and the turret number could also appear on the rear of the turret, where for some reason it was painted in black – perhaps red was used for the overall *Fahrgestell* whereas black indicated a sub-component. Occasionally they were also painted outside (presumably for convenience), usually on the driver's visor, but are only infrequently seen in photographs, probably due to repeated repainting for camouflage purposes. Identification of the *Fahrgestell* number allows the historian to begin to trace the manufacturer and original *Ausfuhrung*.

During the war the British and US technical intelligence staffs spent a lot of time trying to work out who was making the tanks, where the factories were and how many were being made. Assisting them in the task were the manufacturers' marks that many of the bigger companies used on their components. Additionally, codes made up of three letters were to be found on many parts, which was partially decoded during the war and then a final list published in 1946 after the occupation of Germany. These were in use throughout the war but standardised in 1942; mostly stamped or cast in lower case, they were sometimes used in upper-case format to make

identification easier. The larger companies had more than one code allocated; these probably indicated the exact factory or sub-location involved. Recognition of these assisted the Allies in working out exceptionally accurate figures for production based upon captured examples with known numbers, a little-known mathematical feat referred to at the time as the German Tank Problem.

BELOW The 68431 painted in black tells us the number allocated to the turret – not necessarily the same as the *Fahrgestell* number. If it happened to be the same – which did happen – then this tank would be a MIAG-built Ausf J. *(TM 2928/F2)*

TABLE 2C: PRODUCTION AUSFUHRUNG E–N

CONTRACTOR	AUSF	FAHRGESTELL	PRODUCTION	NUMBER	TOTAL	REMARKS
Daimler-Benz	E	60401–60441	Late 1938–July 1939	41	96	Production delayed by transmission production problems. Majority of turrets built by Alkett.
MAN		60442–60496	March–December 1939	55		
MAN	F	61001–61096	September 1939–?	96	435	Production due to delays with: transmission, steering units, tracks, shock absorbers, armour. Alkett production delayed due to *Tauchpanzer* conversions. Last Ausf F with 37mm completed July 1940. Between 75 and 96 completed with 50mm L/42, remainder with 37mm. * Daimler-Benz only completed 45 of the 95 contracted (61145–61189); Henschel completed the remaining 50 before starting their own 120.
Daimler-Benz		61101–61195	November 1939–July 1940	95*		
FAMO		61201–61228	First half of 1940	28		
Henschel		61301–61420	August 1939–mid-1940	120*		
MIAG		61501–61560	September 1939–June 1940	60		
Alkett		61601–61636	January–March 1941	36		
MAN	G	65001–65090	cMarch 1940–early 1941	90	600	Contract reduced from 800 to 600 because of problems with Variorex gearbox. First tank with 50mm L/42 completed July 1940. Between 439 and 458 completed with 50mm L/42, remainder with 37mm. * 6 diverted to Sturmgeschutz production.
Henschel		65101–65255	cMarch 1940–early 1941	155		
FAMO		65365–65379	cMarch 1940–early 1941	15		
Alkett		65401–65550	cMarch 1940–early 1941	150		
MIAG		65720–65799	July–December 1940	80		
Daimler-Benz		65801–65860	April–August 1940	60*		
MNH		65901–65950	cJuly 1940–cMay 1941	50		
Daimler-Benz	H	66001–66050	October 1940–March 1941	50	286	Contract reduced from 759 to 286 in July 1940 in order to increase production of up-armoured models.
MAN		66101–66198	November 1940–March 1941	98		
MIAG		66301–66372	December 1940–April 1941	72		
Henschel		66401–66466	December 1940–March 1941	66		
Daimler-Benz	J	68001–68134	March–September 1941	134	779	Contract increased from 440.
MAN		68201–68333	March–September 1941	133		
MIAG		68401–68533	April–September 1941	133		
MNH		68601–68700	March–August 1941	100		
Henschel		68701–68979	March 1941–January 1942	279		

CONTRACTOR	AUSF	FAHRGESTELL	PRODUCTION	NUMBER	TOTAL	REMARKS
Daimler-Benz		72001–72325	September 1941–June 1942	325		Approximately 110 made with L/42 (Ausf J), remainder with L/60 (c215 Ausf L).
MAN		72401–72725	September 1941–May 1942	325		Approximately 150 made with L/42 (Ausf J), remainder with L/60 (c175 Ausf L).
MIAG		72801–73125	September 1941–May 1942	325		Approximately 110 made with L/42 (Ausf J), remainder with L/60 (c215 Ausf L).
MNH		73201–73525	August 1941–June 1942	325		Approximately 150 made with L/42 (Ausf J), remainder with L/60 (c175 Ausf L).
Henschel		73601–73630 73764–73900	January–August 1942	30 137		All 167 made with L/42 (Ausf J).
Alkett	J, L, M, N	73901–74250	April 1941–October 1942	350	3,235	Approximately 120 made with L/42 (Ausf J), remainder with L/60 (c230 Ausf L).
Daimler-Benz		74251–74350 75101–75230	June–July 1942	100 130		Initial contract was for 130 Ausf J, possibly for FAMO.
MAN		74351–74600	May–October 1942	250		Approximately 180 Ausf L, 70 Ausf M
MIAG		74601–74850	May–September 1942	250		Proportion of Ausf L to Ausf M not known.
MNH		74851–75100	July–October 1942	250		
Henschel		75231–75500	August–September 1942	270		
MIAG		76361–76528	September–December 1942	168		First 18 Ausf L? 76401 onwards probably Ausf M.
MAN		76111–76126	December 1942–January 1943	16		
MNH	M	76211–76278	December 1942–February 1943	68	159	
Daimler-Benz		77534–77543	September–October 1942	10		
MIAG		77544–77608	December 1942	65		
MIAG	N	77709–77793	July–October 1942	185	185	Total Ausf N made 450; therefore c265 within range 72001–76528 above.
TOTAL GUN TANKS					**5,775**	
Daimler-Benz	*Befehls* E	60501–60545	Unknown	45		
Daimler-Benz	*Befehls* H	70001–70175	November 1940–September 1942	175	351	
Henschel	*Befehls* J	73631–73711	August 1942–November 1942	81		
Daimler-Benz	*Befehls* K	70201–70250	December 1942–February 1943	50		
TOTAL COMMAND TANKS					**351**	
MIAG	Flamm M	77609–77708	Unknown	100	100	
TOTAL					**6,226**	

TABLE 2D: EXAMPLE MANUFACTURERS' CODES

Company	Code(s)
Alkett	csg
Bosch	bjp, hbu
FAMO	bvf
Henschel	cvd, dkr, eds, her, hsr
Leitz	beh
MAN	bnd
Maybach	cre, pye
MIAG	bal, emp
Nordbau	nct
Rheinmetall-Borsig	amp, bmv, bwc, cbv, coc, fqv, fxc

Throughout the war the provision of spare parts for tanks was woefully insufficient, as most of the industrial capacity was geared to building weapons and not the spare parts to support them when they broke down. For example, the ratio of tanks to engines made seems to have been around 3:4 – for every three tanks made, there were four engines produced, or one spare engine for every three tanks. Faith in the quality of a product is one thing, but when engines failed more frequently than expected, for example in the dust of North Africa or the terrible cold of Russia, the repair crews would have to resort to cannibalisation – taking parts from other vehicles – to keep tanks going. Similarly, between 1938 and 1943 ZF made 10,074 gearboxes for use on tanks, but of these only 1,468, about 15%, were made as spares – that is one spare gearbox for every six tanks. A similar problem affected the final drives, another component where supply could never meet demand. During the French campaign it was reported that: 'The spare parts for the Panzer III were insufficient. To keep the combat strength of the *Panzer Regimenter* passably high, the tanks often had to run with heavily worn rubber rims, sometimes even without.' On 6 May 1941 the *Deutsches Afrika Korps* (DAK) were already reporting that only 10 to 15% of their spare part requirements were being met. In Russia in October 1941, the 18th Panzer Division recorded that they had lost 59 tanks in action, but another 103 due to the lack of spare parts.

As the war progressed, two external factors combined to force changes to the design of the tank. These were the increasing limitations in the supply of raw materials, and the need to increase production to the maximum possible. This came to a head once Operation Barbarossa became bogged down in the Russian winter, and Hitler decreed to Speer on 3 December 1941 that arms production must be rationalised and speeded up. Therefore, the design of the Panzer III (and other weapons) was re-examined, with a view to eliminating components that were not essential and which would simplify and thus speed up production; one extreme example of this was reducing the number of securing straps holding a fire extinguisher into its bracket from two to one. By the start of 1942 the need to speed up production and save materials had become ever more urgent, and as another example the two-piece front transmission hatches were replaced with a single-piece version, requiring only two hinges rather than four as well as less machining of the hatches. Vision ports around the turret and hull were also deleted, as were the two hull-side escape hatches. The original turret rear included a protruding support for the cupola, which was an unnecessarily complicated design, requiring two shaped plates as well as additional steel and also welding time. Redesigning the rear of the turret solved the problem.

Once it was decided that the 37mm armed Ausf E would represent the first model to go into genuine series production, not surprisingly the *Heereswaffenamt* (Army Weapons Office) wanted to get the tanks into field units as rapidly as possible, but difficulties with production, particularly with the new Variorex transmission, meant that the schedule they proposed could not be met; Panzer III production always lagged well behind what the army required. Production of the Ausf E started in December 1938, seven months later than planned, and by July 1939 only 19 had been completed. By the outbreak of war with Poland, only another 31 had been made. At this time only two firms were involved in the assembly (Daimler-Benz and MAN), and this represents an average of less than three completed tanks per company per month, a staggeringly low total. Things picked up only very slightly after that, and the invasion of Poland meant that the final 35 tanks were completed in two calendar months. A very few brand new Ausf Es had been used by Panzer Regt 3 (part

of the 2nd Panzer Division) in the occupation of
the rump of Czechoslovakia in early 1939, and
earlier models in very low numbers also seem to
have taken part in the Anschluss with Austria in
March 1938 (also 2nd Pz Div), as well as in the
occupation of the Sudetenland in October of the
same year (1st Pz Div). The Ausf F represented
a modest but by no means revolutionary
advance over the E, but critically three more
manufacturers (Alkett, Henschel and FAMO)
were brought into the production scheme for
the type. The new six-wheel suspension used
on the E had been found to be suitable, and
the armour and armament initially remained the
same. Some 435 were built between September
1939 and July 1940, an average of only about
seven tanks per builder per month. The key
improvement was the introduction of the 50mm
L/42 gun on the last 100 Ausf Fs made. This
was of course always the weapon desired for
the tank,[6] and which had proved to be urgently
required by the French campaign, where the
37mm-armed tank was outgunned by both
the British 2-pounder and the French 47mm.
After the conclusion of the French campaign,
Hitler intervened in production policy, ordering
that 800–1,000 Panzer III and IV tanks were to
be built each month. This was pure fantasy as
there was not the capacity to achieve anything
like this amount – in December 1940 the real
output was a mere 102 Panzer IIIs completed.
Aside from the huge financial and raw material
implications, the telling argument was the lack of
skilled workers, with an additional 100,000 being
estimated as necessary – and who of course
would take a long time to train even if they could
be made available. The plan was abandoned.[7]

Another Hitlerian directive issued around the
same time (3 July 1940) using the *Führerprinzip*
was that the Panzer III should be rearmed with
a new gun. This was to be the 50mm L/60 gun,
a tank version of the new PaK 38 and using
the same length barrel but without a muzzle
brake. Without informing Hitler, the 'experts'
(including Porsche) all privately agreed that this

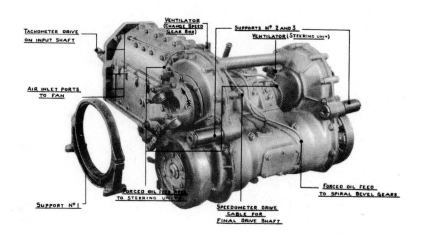

was impossible and so the gun that was actually
fitted was the shorter and therefore less effective
L/42 gun. The reason(s) for the 'impossible' tag
was not stated, but it may well have been to
do with the perceived length of recoil; the PaK
38 had a recoil length of around 22in (559mm)
which could not be accommodated inside the
turret. Apparently, Hitler did not discover that
his order had been ignored until 18 February
1941 during a conference of tank experts at
Berchtesgaden; unsurprisingly he was enraged
that his order had not been followed. The
experts – publicly this time – tried to convince
him that it was technically impossible to fit the
more powerful gun, but a certain Herr Panther (or
Panten, sources disagree) of Alkett volunteered
there and then to build a tank with the bigger
gun, and only two months later this had proved
the concept to be feasible. Therefore, the fitting
of the L/60 began in December 1941, nearly 18
months after the original order. Although it is not
difficult to identify many serious mistakes that
Hitler made throughout the war, this one was not

ABOVE The initially
troublesome and
complicated Variorex
gearbox, which was
fitted with a number of
gears that were all but
unusable in service.

6   In terms of calibre but not barrel length.
7   There was a stark choice that had to be made between the competing
manpower demands of the Wehrmacht and the industrialists who were
trying to keep it equipped. The Wehrmacht raised its strength from 1.13
million men in the summer of 1939 to 4.55 million by the end of the year,
and drafted another million over Christmas. Included in this were 1.3
million experienced industrial workers.

of his making; had the Panzer III been equipped with the longer gun as ordered, the T34 might not have had quite such an impact when it was first encountered. The whole episode was clearly important, as Hitler frequently referred to it in later years as an example of how army intransigence had wrecked his carefully considered plans. Because of the delay caused by the disobedience, by the time it was fitted the L/60 was already on the verge of being outclassed in Russia (although not yet in North Africa). On 1 July 1941 it was reported that the German army held 327 Panzer IIIs with the 37mm gun, and 1,174 with the 50mm (all L/42). By April 1942 the totals were 131 and 1,893 respectively; clearly the production of new tanks plus the rearming of older models was shifting the balance away from the smaller calibre – but the majority of the 50mm tanks were still armed with the L/42.

When the nature of warfare on the Eastern Front changed from largely offensive operations to those which were essentially defensive, the types of vehicles required also changed, and Albert Speer (never a completely reliable witness) complained during interrogation that the German generals never understood the need to match the weapons produced to the type of fighting. Under interrogation in 1945, Herr Kurt Arnoldt, Henschel's chief technical engineer, complained that 'Hitler took a great personal interest in AFV design although he knew nothing about it.' He went on to state that the three most malignant influences on German tank design were Hitler, Speer and Porsche. In his opinion all three were drawn towards the 'grandiose' at the expense of the effective. He wasn't the only one to complain of interference from outside: another German engineer interviewed after the war reported that 'Guderian complained that [tank] development work had largely ceased [by mid-1941] because Hitler was convinced that the war was effectively over.' The shift in the type of tank needed occurred at the time when Germany was beginning to discover just how difficult it was to produce all the myriad of weapons (and ammunition, and fuel, spare parts, etc.) that it needed, as well as trying to develop more advanced ones. In defensive situations the amount of armour on a tank and particularly its gun power became more important than its mobility, and this formula was the death knell of the Panzer III which had been built with mobility as its prime characteristic at the expense of armour. Over two years of combat it had been developed and improved as far as it could be: the armour had been successfully thickened and the gun replaced twice, but there was nowhere left for it to go as a battle tank.[8] It could still provide useful service as a support tank for Tigers, and its successful chassis would continue to be used as the basis of the Sturmgeschutz III[9] assault gun, around three of which could be built for every two gun tanks, and so the last Panzer III gun tank was built in August 1943.

The gun tanks: *Ausfuhrung E–N*

At this juncture it is appropriate to make an important point about the *Ausfuhrung* system. Because of the way that changes were introduced during production (and bearing in mind that there were seven different firms often building different models of the tanks at different, sometimes overlapping, periods) it is unwise to try to be too dogmatic about which

RIGHT A lubrication and maintenance book for chassis No 72878, a tank built by MIAG in late 1941. This book formed part of the tank's manuals and the instruction at the top told the crew to leave it in the tank, but it is notable that the same instructions applied to Ausf E–J inclusive, indicating how similar the various models were in many respects.

D 652/28

72878   6/18

Zum Einlegen in das Gerät!

Panzerkampfwagen III

Ausf. E bis J

Fristenheft
für
Schmieren und Pflegearbeiten
zum
Fahrgestell Nr. 72878

Heft 1

von 250 km bis 4000 km

Vom 20. 7. 41

Berlin 1941

Gedruckt bei der Ernst Steiniger Druck- und Verlagsanstalt

8   A British report was complimentary when it concluded that 'The history of the Panzer III is a remarkable example of what can be done to improve the armour protection of an AFV without fundamentally altering its design.'
9   The story of these successful and prolific vehicles will be covered in detail in a future Haynes Manual.

models displayed which features, particularly with the ones that could be swapped between tanks fairly easily. Field repairs and the provision of upgrade kits (*Schürzen*, *Vorpanzer,* etc.) also played their part, and a study of photographs often reveal tanks which are a kind of hybrid; for example, it was quite possible to remove a damaged turret from one tank and replace it with a serviceable one from a different tank with a damaged hull. A German instruction issued in September 1940 ordered that around 600 early models were to be brought up to the latest specification, including rearming with 50mm guns, modifying MG34s for belt feed, adding additional armour and replacing the torsion bars, among others; such tanks would therefore display a mix of early and late features, depending on their initial *Ausfuhrung.* After examining a number of captured tanks, British experts quickly realised that the style and location of any extra armour plates fitted did not necessarily depend upon the original *Ausfuhrung.* Additionally, even the most diligent researchers who have tried to identify the features particular to each model often disagree. Therefore the explanations of which models had which features must be used as a guide to the 90% solution – there will often be exceptions to the rule. Another problem we will come to in due course concerns the amalgamation and lack of clarity over the last contracts, particularly affecting Ausf J onwards.

AUSF E

The first example of an Ausf E was only accepted into service in late 1938 owing to production being delayed by gearbox problems; by June 1939 only 19 had been accepted into service and only around 50 by the outbreak of war with Poland. The new torsion bar suspension had a shorter length of track in contact with the ground than the early models, by about 80cm, which raised the ground pressure and meant that the tanks were less able to deal with muddy conditions despite the improved ride. The original intention was for the first tank to be completed in May 1938 and the last one only four months later in September. Delays on gearbox production at Maybach meant that in fact the first one was not accepted until December 1938; in May 1939

AUSF E SPECIFICATIONS	
Series code	4/ZW
Engine	Maybach HL 120 TR, a bored-out version of the earlier HL 108. This increased the power to 265hp.
Gearbox	Maybach Variorex ten-speed and reverse pre-select. This was adopted in an attempt to allow the tank to travel at up to 70kph on roads, hence the use of ten gears. The unit proved to be unnecessarily complicated, and its top gears were all but unusable. High speeds also damaged the roadwheel tyres and drivers were instructed not to exceed 40kph, negating the need for the ten gears.
Steering	Hydraulic, differential clutch and brake.
Suspension	A completely new suspension system was adopted with all wheels operating independently, and a Porsche-engineered torsion bar design was adopted, with six medium-sized roadwheels which had superior service life. Vertical shock absorbers were fitted to wheels one and six.
Tracks	360mm, 93 links per side. Rubber-padded lubricated tracks were envisaged for the tank to facilitate a high road speed, but were not proceeded with as they were very heavy and the pads were difficult to secure.
Power to weight (hp per ton)	13.6
Armour protection	
Hull maximum	30mm face-hardened.
Hull minimum	30mm sides, 20mm rear. Belly and engine deck 16mm.
Turret maximum	30mm mantlet, front and sides.
Turret minimum	16mm roof.
Additional	None.
Armament	
Main gun	37mm L/45.
Ammunition	125 rounds.
Secondary armament	2 × MG34 (turret), 1 × MG34 (hull) in *Kugelblende 30.* 4,500 rounds 7.92mm in 60 double drum magazines of 75 rounds.
Other features	Single fuel tank (310 litres) to right of engine with 8mm armour. Hull escape hatches fitted both sides between first and second top rollers. Driver's *Fahrersehklappe 30* twin-block rise and fall visor, and *Fahreroptik* KFF1 ×1.15 binocular periscope used when the visor was closed. Horn moved to right trackguard.
Recognition features	Internal mantlet with short gun. Six roadwheels. Twin turret side doors. No turret rear bin. Two-piece driver's visor. Flat engine decks with hatches replaced louvres used on Ausf A–D.

RIGHT An Ausf E with the typical sprocket and idler designs used on the early service tanks, each having eight 'holes'.

BELOW The Maybach HL 120 TR front view (left) and rear (right).

ABOVE Side view of the TR engine. The TR used twin Bosch SR6 magnetos, which proved to be troublesome and the cause of difficult starting.

BELOW The early-style flat engine decks and turret roof with two circular signal ports, plus the angled turret ring deflector plates fitted to the roof of the superstructure.

production ground to a halt as no gearboxes were available.[10] Eventually all tanks were completed by the end of 1939, which included MAN producing their first 55 Panzer IIIs.

AUSF F

The Ausf F was very similar to the Ausf E, and was the first model to be selected for something approaching mass production. Because of the introduction of the L/42 gun during production, there were two distinct varieties of Ausf F: about 330–350 were made with the 37mm, and up to 100 with the 50mm. Three additional companies were brought into the production scheme: Henschel, Alkett and FAMO. The majority of the tanks made after July 1940 were fitted with the 50mm L/42 gun, with

10 As a result of the initial problems encountered with the gearbox, the Weapons Office decided to reintroduce the ZF type into the Panzer III. However, the Variorex production had reached about 1,400 units, which then had to be used up before the ZF SSG 77 Aphon could be introduced on the Ausf H.

ABOVE The slightly modified Maybach TRM engine. At 2,600rpm the unit delivered 265hp, rising to a maximum of 300hp at 3,000rpm (and which is why some references disagree on the amount of power the engine delivered).

AUSF F SPECIFICATIONS	
Series code	5/ZW
Engine	Maybach HL 120 TRM, which was the TR with a single Bosch JO12 114 magneto system and modified cooling. Output 285hp.
Power to weight (hp per ton)	14.6
Armour protection	
Turret	The 50mm gun mantlet maximum thickness was increased to 35mm.
Additional	Three angled deflector plates fitted to superstructure top to protect turret ring.
Armament	
Main gun	37mm L/45. Tanks completed after July 1940 had 50mm L/42 in an external mantlet.
Ammunition	125 rounds (37mm), 99 rounds (50mm). From June 1940 MG34 converted from drum to belt feed.
Other features	Steering brake air vents (cowls) introduced during production. Wider tyres (95mm, previously 75mm) fitted from May 1940 to extend tyre life. Photographs show that some tanks were fitted with a mix of the old and new, an example of poor control during production. Front top roller moved slightly forward from September 1940. Side visor added for radio operator on some tanks. Notek front and rear convoy lights added from March 1940.
Recognition features	Internal mantlet with short gun (37mm) and twin coax, or external mantlet with L/42 50mm KwK38 gun and single coax. Smoke discharger system fitted to hull rear.

sighting equipment and ammunition stowage altered to suit; 99 rounds of main armament ammunition were carried and only one coax MG was fitted in an external mantlet. The first tank was completed in August 1939, but delays in the supply of armoured components – and in Alkett's case the distraction of converting other tanks into diving tanks (*Tauchpanzer*) – meant production did not cease until spring 1941.

AUSF G

This was another evolutionary stage in the design which was produced concurrently with the earlier Ausf F and later H. MIAG and MNH were brought into the production scheme. The Ausf G was built between March 1940 and early 1941. Initially 800 were meant to be produced (one source states 1,250), but this was then reduced to 600 – see Ausf J. Around 150 of the

BELOW A 21st Panzer Division Ausf G knocked out and captured in North Africa.

AUSF G SPECIFICATIONS	
Series code	6a/ZW (37mm), 6b/ZW (50mm)
Engine	Maybach HL 120 TRM.
Gearbox	Maybach Variorex ten-speed and reverse pre-select. The earlier problems with the gearbox were largely resolved by the time it was fitted to Ausf G, making it much more reliable.
Suspension	Improved track tensioner and larger shock absorbers.
Armour protection	
Additional	From late 1940, additional flush-fitting 30mm plates were designed to be bolted on to the driver's front vertical plate, as well as the hull front and rear. A lack of these plates meant that not all tanks were fitted with the hull plates during production, but bolts were provided to allow them to be mounted when available.
Armament	
Main gun	37mm L/45. Tanks completed after July 1940 had the 50mm L/42 in an external mantlet.
Ammunition	125 rounds (37mm), 99 rounds (50mm).
Other features	Revised driver's *Drehsehklappe* – pivoting visor. Driver's *Fahreroptik* KFF2 ×1.15 binocular prismatic periscope used when the visor was closed.
Recognition features	External starter cover on hull rear now cast and hinged at top. Single-piece driver's visor. Turret rear bin on some (from April 1941). Single signal flag flap in turret roof (RHS). Turret ventilator forward and left of cupola or in front centre of roof. Tool box and spare roadwheel mount fitted to trackguards.

tanks were made with the 37mm gun, a few as late as September 1940, but the majority were built with the 50mm L/42. A revised cupola with increased protection was fitted to some tanks, and a 12 o'clock turret position indicator system was mounted for the use of the commander and gunner. The left signal flag flap in the turret roof was deleted and an electric turret gun ventilator fan was mounted in the roof to the front of the cupola; this necessitated a modification to the gun guard of the main armament to prevent it being fouled on the internal fan guard when in depression. This then led to the relocation of the fan further forward and above the gun breeches, with a circular plate used to close the hole in front of the cupola. The vision flaps in the turret side hatches were redesigned.

AUSF H

The Ausf H was the first model designed to mount a 50mm L/42 gun *ab initio*. The design – which had actually been ordered in January 1939 and completed before the war started – was also used as the start point when converting 37mm-armed tanks to the larger gun. The original intention was to make the Ausf H similar in other respects to the G, but the need to change the gearbox and add extra armour led to further modifications. Some 759 Ausf Hs were ordered in July 1938, with contracts issued in the following summer. Planning assumed that deliveries were to

RIGHT A brand new Ausf H with the circular hull MG mounting and new pattern sprockets and idlers.

ABOVE AND BELOW The new design of idler and sprocket, used from the Ausf H onwards.

AUSF H	
Series code	7/ZW
Gearbox	The Maybach Variorex, although improved, had fallen out of favour and was replaced by the new ZF SSG 77 Aphon. This was a synchronised manual six forward and reverse unit.
Suspension	A widened suspension was fitted, consisting of a new sprocket, idlers, wider roadwheels and 380mm track. Due to supply problems some were fitted with old-style sprockets and idlers with spacers; others had the early type of shock absorber. The top roller mounts were modified to place the centre of the wheels in the correct position.
Tracks	380mm or 400mm.
Power to weight (hp per ton)	13.3
Armament	
Main gun	50mm L/42 in external mantlet.
Ammunition	99 rounds. 3,750 rounds of 7.92mm.
Other features	Modified turret rear with no welded bulge. Gun balance achieved by a removable counterweight fitted to the recoil guard. Some were modified for tropical (*Tropen*) use (starting January/February 1941) or winterised for Russia (all from 1 September 1942 – see Ausf L and M).
Recognition features	50mm L/42 gun. Turret bin as standard (fitted post-production). Widened suspension components. New sprocket and idler design. Single-piece turret rear plate. Larger gap between rear of turret hatches and turret rear than previously.

start in October 1940 and be complete by September 1941. The ammunition load for the 50mm gun was meant to consist of mostly HE shells – 58 *Sprengpatronen*, plus 36 AP shells (which left space for another five of either AP or HE at the crew's discretion); this may seem a strange mix for a tank that was still, officially at least, the primary battle tank, but shows how dangerous the dug-in anti-tank gun menace was perceived to be. To simplify production the turret was redesigned slightly, with the rear plate being made from a single curved plate, requiring the cupola to be moved forward slightly.

RIGHT This is an Ausf L, but shows the new single curved rear plate used on the turret from the Ausf H to simplify production.

AUSF J SPECIFICATIONS	
Series code	8/ZW
Engine	Maybach HL 120 TRM.
Gearbox	ZF SSG 77 Aphon.
Steering	Mechanical.
Tracks	380mm or 400mm, some with slots on the outside faces to take removable ice cleats.
Power to weight (hp per ton)	13.2
Armour protection	
Hull maximum	50mm face-hardened front and rear.
Hull minimum	30mm sides. Belly and engine deck 16mm.
Turret maximum	57mm trunnion cheek armour. 50mm mantlet, 30mm front and sides. Not all tanks were fitted with the thicker mantlet; early versions built had the previous type.
Turret minimum	16mm roof.
Armament	
Main gun	50mm L/42.
Ammunition	99 rounds.
Other features	Thicker torsion bars – front three 55mm diameter, rear three 52mm. Improved oil bath air filtration.
Recognition features	Lengthened hull with integral front towing eyes. Revised driver's *Fahrersehklappe 50* pivoting visor. *Kugelblende 50* hull MG mount. One-piece front hinged hatches on nose. Improved brake cooling cowls. Small tool box mounted on front right trackguard. Turret ventilation fan mounted directly above main armament/coax breeches. Spare roadwheel pair carried front and rear of the left trackguard with revised external tool stowage as a result. L/42 gun does not protrude past hull front. Smoke dischargers located under hull rear overhang.

AUSF J

The major improvement in the J model was the use of single 50mm-thick armour plates on the hull front and rear, replacing the 30mm + 30mm configuration used from the Ausf G.[11] A thickened mantlet was used with an extra 20mm of armour inside, so that the outside profile remained the same. However, this meant that a 13mm-deep curved cut-out had to be made in the base to give clearance for the turret ring. The new hull armour necessitated a change in the design of the driver's visor and the hull MG mounting to fit into the thicker plates. As of 1 April 1940 there were still over 2,100 Panzer IIIs of various *Ausfuhrung* on order that had not yet been built; as a result no further orders were placed after the initial Ausf J order until the backlog had started to clear. As a result of these delays in production many of the tanks originally ordered as Ausf G (about 200) and Ausf H (just under 500) were built to Ausf J (or later) standard, with the thicker plates and other modifications. *Fahrgestell* numbers 68001–69100 inclusive were allocated exclusively for Ausf Js built with the L/42 gun – see Table 2E. In total, this amounted to 779 tanks; these were made starting in March 1941 and production generally finished in August/ September 1941, although Henschel production of the J did not end until January 1942. In total around 820 Ausf Js seem to have been made.

---

11 A single 50mm plate would give about the same protection as two 30mm plates bolted together – armour design is not just about the total thickness.

BELOW A destroyed Ausf J in North Africa – an internal explosion has completely removed the turret roof and cupola. *(TM 18/E1)*

BELOW Additional plates were added to the 50mm mantlet ready to take 20mm-thick spaced armour, but many tanks were fielded in this configuration without the extra plate being mounted.

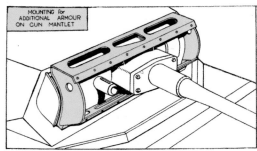

TABLE 2E:
AUSF J PRODUCTION

Daimler-Benz		68001–68134
MAN		68201–68333
MIAG	J	68401–68533
MNH		68601–68700
Henschel		68701–68979

Note: around 50 other Ausf Js were made outside these numbers.

AUSF L AND M

And now we run into a problem: from Ausf J production onwards we start to encounter uncertainty as to which *Fahrgestell* number was issued to which *Ausfuhrung*. Identified in Table

ABOVE The MG34 mounted with the canvas *Gurtsack* ammunition belt holder; here the gun is being used in the ground defence role but it could elevate to about 80° for AA use. The electrical firing cable for the turret smoke dischargers is coiled around the front turret hook.

BELOW The smoke grenade dischargers were mounted using the hook on the turret side. This photograph is of an Ausf N in Tunisia, used in its new role to provide fire support to the less manoeuvrable Tiger. *(Tank Museum)*

ABOVE Ausf L with the *lang* KwK39 50mm gun, thicker armour on the hull front and original mantlet with no provision for appliqué armour. This tank has the front turret visors, and is probably one of those ordered as a J but renamed when fitted with the L/60 gun.

ABOVE An Ausf L with the framework for a frontal plate to be fitted on the mantlet, toolbox on the right-hand trackguard and the MG34 anti-aircraft mounting on the cupola. The front turret visors have been deleted to simplify production.

BELOW Ausf M with turret smoke grenade dischargers and Bosch headlamps on the trackguards. Note how the L/60 protrudes past the front of the hull.

TABLE 2F: AUSF J–N PRODUCTION

MAKER	AUSF	RANGE	Possible AUSF J	Known AUSF L	Possible AUSF L	Possible AUSF M
Daimler-Benz		72001–72325	72001–72082 (82)	72083–72325 (243)		
MAN		72401–72725	72401–72506 (106)	72507–72725 (219)		
MIAG		72801–73125	72801–72873 (73)	72874–73125 (252)		
MNH		73201–73525	73201–73284 (84)	73285–73525 (241)		
Henschel		73601–73900	73601–73767 (167)	73768–73900 (133)		
Alkett		73901–74250	73901–74012 (112)	74013–74100 (88)	74101–74250 (150)	
Daimler-Benz		74251–74350 75101–75230			74340–74350 (11) 75221–75230 (10)	
MAN	J, L, M, N	74351–74600			74351–74530 (180)	74531–74600 (70)
MIAG		74601–74850			74601–74850 (250)	
MNH		74851–75100			74851–75000 (150)	75001–75100 (100)
Henschel		75231–75500			75237–75370 (134)	75371–75430 (60)
Alkett		74101–74250			74101–74250 (250)	
MAN		76111–76126				76111–76126 (16)
MNH		76211–76278*				76211–76278 (68)
MIAG		76361–76528				76401–76528 (128)
Daimler-Benz		77534–77543				77534–77543 (10)
MIAG		77544–77608				77544–77608 (65)

Note: *56 Panzer IIIs built for export to Turkey within this range (76223–76278).*

2F are 3,235 tanks which could be anything from the final Ausf Js to be built, through Ausf L to M or N, although it is not always clear which ones were which. The Germans were more concerned in labelling their tanks according to the gun carried than any other feature, and therefore late production tanks ordered as Ausf J but delivered with the L/60 became Ausf L.

Ausf L production began with 40 tanks completed in December 1941. Contracts were placed for the Ausf M in February 1942. Both the Ausf L and M were armed – finally – with the L/60 50mm gun. All manufacturers other than Henschel started production of L/60 tanks in December 1941, but Henschel did not commence production until May 1942; their production was slowed down by the need to send partially completed tanks to Wegmann for turret installation. During the Ausf L production run, starting in April 1942, both side vision ports on the turret and the loader's observation aperture in the mantlet were deleted in order to simplify production, although existing supplies

RIGHT The rubber plugs fitted to make the steering brake air intakes watertight, plus the welded bar to retain track links on the glacis (green).

FAR RIGHT Ausf M modified rear hull with raised silencer box and sealing flaps. A trailer-towing point was added to some late models.

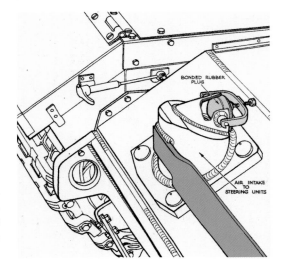

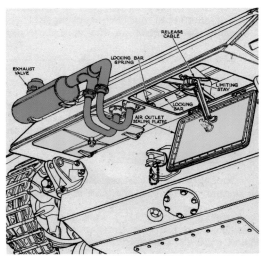

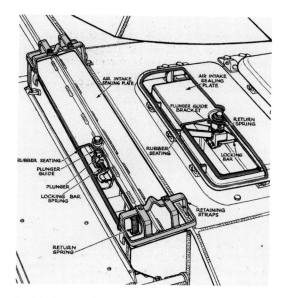

had to be used up and the older components were still being fitted as late as July. For the same reason the scalloped edges on the hull top were replaced with straight-edged angled steel, and both of the hull escape hatches were deleted. Hulls with these features were first made in June 1942 and by October all new tanks were being made with them. Front side lights and the horn were also deleted; from September 1942 Bosch headlamps that were able to be dismounted were fitted on to the trackguards (rather than directly on to the hull), and the Notek driving light was removed. The rear convoy/tail light was replaced by a simplified cylindrical lamp. All tanks built after August 1942 were fitted with special and much-needed cold-weather equipment, including a hot coolant transfer apparatus, a coolant blow-torch heater and a carburettor starter fluid injector system.

Ausf M also featured modifications designed to increase the ability of the tank to wade in deep water; this requirement must have come about as a result of experience gained in Russia during 1941. The brake ventilation cowls were fitted with rubber bungs, the exhaust system at the rear was raised up and fitted with a one-way valve and all hatches and other apertures and fittings on the hull and turret were sealed, mostly with rubber gaskets.

The Ausf K was never produced as a gun tank, although the designation was used for 50 *Befehlspanzer* made by Daimler-Benz (see p. 57).

ABOVE LEFT Sealing arrangements on the engine deck cowls – the retaining straps (yellow) were used to push the sealing plates down against the rubber gaskets on the side air intake louvres.

ABOVE Two Ausf Ms in action in Kursk 1943, with the new exhaust layout clearly visible.

AUSF L AND M SPECIFICATIONS	
Series code	8/ZW
Engine	Maybach HL 120 TRM.
Gearbox	ZF SSG 77 Aphon.
Steering	Mechanical.
Power to weight (hp per ton)	12.7
Armour protection	
Hull maximum	50mm face-hardened front and rear.
Hull minimum	30mm sides. Belly and engine deck 16mm.
Turret maximum	57mm trunnion cheek armour. 50mm mantlet, 30mm front and sides. Not all tanks were fitted with the thicker mantlet; some early versions had the previous type.
Turret minimum	16mm roof.
Armament	
Main gun	50mm L/60.
Ammunition	84 rounds (46 *SprGr*, 30 *PzGr*, 8 optional).
Recognition features	L/60 gun protrudes past hull front. Turret side visors and loader's vision port on mantlet deleted on some, possibly most. Single-piece front hull hatches. No Notek light, horn or sidelights. Bosch headlamps on trackguards. Triple-barrel turret smoke grenade dischargers fitted to both sides from September 1942; fitting ceased May 1943. Hull escape hatches and hull smoke dischargers deleted.

AUSF N SPECIFICATIONS	
Series code	8/ZW
Engine	Maybach HL 120 TRM.
Gearbox	ZF SSG 77 Aphon.
Steering	Mechanical.
Tracks	380mm or 400mm, some with slots on the outsides to take removable ice cleats.
Power to weight (hp per ton)	12.4
Armour protection	
Hull maximum	50mm face-hardened front and rear.
Hull minimum	30mm sides. Belly and engine deck 16mm.
Turret maximum	57mm trunnion cheek armour. 50mm mantlet, 30mm front and sides.
Turret minimum	16mm roof.
Armament	
Main gun	75mm L/24.
Ammunition	64 rounds.
Recognition features	Stubby L/24 gun in an external mantlet.

AUSF N

The decision to produce a fire support version of the Panzer III mounting the L/24 75mm gun was taken in February 1942, with 450 required to be built; these were known as the Ausf N. The Ausf N was often equipped with old L/24 guns taken from Panzer IVs, but in most respects should be considered as a new build and not a conversion. Two new SdKfz designations had to be introduced by the ordnance services to differentiate those tanks fitted with the L/60 or

LEFT A captured Ausf N with *Schürzen* in Russia, c1943. (*TM 2358/A3*)

BELOW An Ausf N with the commander's gun pointer visible in front of the cupola and the external cowl for the ventilator fan in front of it. The gunner's armoured visor is open.

BELOW A great view of an Ausf N captured in Tunisia. This might well be the example which is now in the Tank Museum, Bovington. If so, it was built by MNH and shipped to Bizerte in January 1943. When captured it belonged to Heavy Tank Battalion 501.

L/24 guns; those with the L/60 became the SdKfz 141/1, and 75mm-armed Ausf N tanks were the SdKfz 141/2.

The variants

PanzerBefehlsWagen (Command tank)

It should come as no surprise to discover that a large number of Panzer IIIs were made in the guise of command tanks; it appears that over 350 were made in all. Just like the British, the Germans realised that effective control of large armoured formations required leaders to be up at the front with the troops, where they were best placed to see and exploit opportunities: this was one of the real strengths of Blitzkrieg. Nearly 200 Panzer I Ausf Bs had been converted into command vehicles (*KleinesBefehlsWagen*), but they suffered a number of significant disadvantages: they were extremely lightly armoured (even after appliqué was fitted) and armed, and were different to the tanks that they were commanding, which was poor from the logistic, mobility and protection perspectives. What was needed were command tanks based on the new battle tank, the Panzer III. The first order for *PanzerBefehlsWagen III* (armoured command vehicle) was placed in October 1935, but the first two examples were not ready for service until late 1938. These were built by – or converted into – command vehicles by Daimler-Benz who had taken the lead on the design, assisted by Krupp. The designation of these tanks can be quite confusing to understand, but is actually quite simple. There are two ways of classifying the command tanks. This first is to consider them as the *Ausfuhrung* that they were

based upon, which determines their general configuration, including mobility, hull and turret features, and armament. The second is to classify them into the role they were fitted out for, in other words their radio equipment. This second option is much neater as it used the SdKfz system:

- SdKfz 266   *PanzerBefehlsWagen* (FuG 6 and FuG 2 radios). Battalion HQ vehicle
- SdKfz 267   *PanzerBefehlsWagen* (FuG 6 and FuG 8 radios). Regimental HQ vehicle
- SdKfz 268   *PanzerBefehlsWagen* (FuG 6 and FuG 7 radios). Divisional HQ vehicle.

FuG 2 was the receiver-only part of the FuG 5, operating in the VHF band and using the normal 2m antenna.[12] FuG 6 was in effect a higher-powered version of the FuG 5 produced specifically for tank units; it was a 20W set operating in the same 27.2 to 33.3MHz range and also used the 2m rod aerial. FuG 7 worked in the 42.1 to 47.8MHz range, and was used with a 1.4m rod antenna for ground-to-air communications with reconnaissance aircraft carrying the FuG 17 set. FuG 8 was the main divisional level MW radio, which today would be regarded as HF (high frequency). It worked between 1.13 to 3.00MHz with a 30W output and had a range of about 25km when mobile (double that when stationary), and was used with either the frame or the star antenna – see

---

12 Why a command vehicle would use a receiver only rather than the FuG 5 with transmitter is not clear, unless the radios listed are *additional to* the standard FuG 5; this would make sense in terms of the antennae fitted to the command tank, each one having three different antennae mounted.

ABOVE An Ausf D¹ with the very distinctive rail aerial fitted over the engine decks, making it an SdKfz 267. Note the different style of side air-intake to those used on the service tanks from Ausf E onwards; this seems to have been a particular feature of the D¹ variant.

BELOW Pre-war: two crewmen wearing the distinctive Schutzmütze headdress, which resembled a floppy beret but concealed a 15mm thick rubber or sponge crash helmet. It was abolished in January 1941. The Ausf D¹ behind shows the antenna base on the left side of the hull which folded forwards when not in use.

later in this chapter. Different antennae were used with these radio sets, according to the radios fitted. Rather than the single antenna mount used by the gun tanks on the right side of the hull, the command variants had two pivoting rod antennae, one mounted on each side of the superstructure, and the early versions of the SdKfz 267 also had a very obvious *Rahmenantenne* (rail or frame) antenna mounted on five vertical wooden posts over the engine decks.[13] The cable for this entered the turret via a porcelain insulator with an armoured cover fitted in the turret right rear. Some vehicles, including the later models of the SdKfz 267 without the *Rahmenantenne*, carried a telescopic elevating 9m *Kurbelmast*

---

13 The British sometimes nicknamed this the 'clothes rail' antenna.

8 aerial used for longer-range communication when static, and which may have been able to be elevated through the signal port in the turret roof. Cable drums for field telephones were reported as being required, though these are rarely visible in most photographs.

Five different *Ausfuhrung* were built: D¹, E, H, J and K. The earliest was the D¹, based upon but not identical to the Ausf D gun tank, this was probably a decision forced upon the army by the delayed production of the Ausf E gun tanks, necessitating the use of an inferior chassis but better than no tank at all. Thirty were built, with the first two (belatedly) coming into service by 1 October 1938, another 26 by 20 February 1939, and production was complete by March 1939. Some 24 were built as SdKfz 267, and the other six as SdKfz 268 (with no rail antenna) – at this stage the SdKfz 266 for the battalion commander was either not required, was not top priority, or was thought of as being adequately addressed by the Panzer I *Befehlswagen*. A rod antenna was mounted to the right-hand front of the superstructure, pivoting rearwards, with a second rod on the left-hand side rear, pivoting forwards. Owing to their vulnerability on the battlefield they were up-armoured to 30mm frontal, the same as the standard Ausf E. One unique feature of the D¹ was that there was only one transmission access hatch on the nose (on the driver's side), and photographic evidence indicates that the air intakes on the engine decks may have been of a different design (more akin to those on the Panzer IV) than on the standard Ausf D.

The Ausf E-based command tank carried a maximum of 30mm of frontal armour and thus was no better protected than the first version, but used the improved six-roadwheel suspension of the later models; the driver's visor was altered to a two-piece pivoting design. It carried the same dummy 37mm gun as the D¹ and 45 were built in all. Next came the Ausf H version, with 175 being built in two batches. This had improved armour, with 30mm appliqué being used to double the frontal protection, and the dummy mantlet and gun were made to resemble the newly introduced L/42. The cupola was also modified with narrower visor covers than previously. The Ausf J was introduced in response to reports – complaints – regarding the vulnerability of the tanks armed with

TABLE 2G: *BEFEHLSWAGEN* PRODUCTION

Ausfuhrung	Fahrgestell	No built	Production dates	Features and remarks
D[1]	60341–60370	30	September 1938–March 1939	Based on Ausf D, but with single transmission access hatch on glacis in front of driver. Fixed turret, 30mm frontal armour, dummy 37mm gun. Single-piece driver's visor. Built by Daimler-Benz. Configured as SdKfz 267 and 268.
E	60501–60545	45	July 1939–February 1940	Hull similar to Ausf E. Fixed turret, 30mm frontal armour, dummy 37mm gun. Two-part pivoting driver's visor. Built by Daimler-Benz. Configured as SdKfz 266, 267 or 268.
H	70001–70145	145	November 1940–September 1941	Based on Ausf H, made in two batches. Fixed turret, 30mm frontal armour plus 30mm appliqué, dummy 50mm gun. Two-part pivoting driver's visor. Modified cupola. Built by Daimler-Benz. Configured as SdKfz 266, 267 or 268.
	70146–70175	30	December 1941–January 1942	
J	73631–73763	81	February 1942–April 1942	The contract covered 132 vehicles, so the last chassis made was probably 73711. Based on Ausf J, armed with 50mm L/42 gun in rotating turret; no coax MG or rail antenna. Single-piece transmission access hatches. Built by Henschel, converted by Daimler-Benz August–November 1942. Turret smoke dischargers retro-fitted from September 1942, *Schürzen* from May 1943.
K	70201–70250	50	December 1942–February 1943	Order reduced from 80 to 50. Fully rotating turret based on Panzer IV with adaptor ring with L/60 gun (65 rounds) and distinctive narrow mantlet; no coax. No rail antenna. New single-hatch cupola, turret smoke dischargers as standard, *Schürzen* retro-fitted from May 1943.

dummy guns, and featured a fully rotating turret with the L/42 gun and 20mm of appliqué armour on the mantlet, although not surprisingly less main armament ammunition (75 rounds) could be carried than in a gun tank. The rail antenna on the engine decks could not be used with a rotating turret, so the *Sternantenne* (which was 1.3m high and mounted using an antenna base welded on to the rear central engine decks, with four spokes each 600mm long forming the distinctive star shape) was fitted instead. This configuration replaced the earlier frame antenna from the middle of 1942.

The final version was the extremely interesting Ausf K, based upon the failed gun tank of the same designation which was an attempt to mount the larger Panzer IV turret on to a Panzer III hull. Although this did not come into service as a gun tank (with the probable intention of allowing the Panzer III to carry the long 75mm gun), 50 were built as *Befehlswagen* with the L/60 50mm gun in a very distinctive narrow mantlet with a vision port on the right-hand side, but no MG34; only 65 rounds were carried. Some 36 of these tanks were produced in December 1942, 13 in January 1943 and the final example the following month, all at

Daimler-Benz. The modified Panzer IV turret was mounted using an adaptor ring to the Panzer III Ausf M hull, fitted with the usual deep wading modifications and with no side escape hatches. The engine-mounted *Sternantenne* was used, along with two rod antennae, one mounted on the superstructure left rear, the other front right. Interestingly, but a little confusingly, a British report from North Africa noted the mention of an Ausf K command tank in a captured document as early as November 1941, 13 months before it went into production. ...

BELOW Another D[1], this time on a (captured) Polish railway flat in 1939.

ABOVE Another SdKfz 267 *Befehlspanzer* III this time based on an Ausf E – it has the early rectangular cover for the starting handle, as well as the early suspension and narrow tracks. Notice how the antenna cable enters the turret rear using a cable with a flap protecting the porcelain insulator.

ABOVE RIGHT The Star antenna is visible on this *Schürzen*-equipped tank – note also the large box fitted to the front trackguard.

Although the interiors of each model varied according to the radios carried, in many ways they were similar in internal layout and design features. The crew consisted of the commander,[14] driver and radio operator as normal, but the gunner and loader were replaced in the turret with a second radio operator and the commander's adjutant (staff officer) who also manned the turret MG (where fitted). An aluminium dummy gun barrel was fitted externally,[15] so defensively the Ausf D[1]–H relied on the turret-mounted MG34 for self-protection, for which 2,400 rounds were carried. Early versions carried 32 of the unpopular 75-round *doppeltrommel* – double drum magazines, later converted to normal belt feed, with 16 belts of

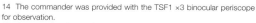

14 The commander was provided with the TSF1 ×3 binocular periscope for observation.
15 An example of wastefulness in the use of materials – why not use wood?

150 rounds in the *gurtsack* canvas containers. A signal pistol with a large number of cartridges was carried as a back-up to the radios. Additionally, three MP38/40s were carried, which could be fired through conical pistol ports in the superstructure. These ports were similar in design to those used in the turret rear, with one replacing the hull MG mounting and the other two fitted to the sides, behind the vision ports. On those tanks fitted with a dummy gun, the turret front plate was replaced by a single armour plate, with a false mantlet made from a cast alloy.

A British report on a captured Ausf H concluded that all the radio equipment had been located in the right side of the turret and fighting compartment, leaving the left side clear for the commander's use, presumably meaning documents, maps and personal kit; writing desks/map tables were provided for the commander and adjutant. The seats were

RIGHT *Schürzen* were retrofitted to *Befehlswagen* from May 1943, by which time the numbers in service were diminishing quite rapidly. The long L/60 is very distinctive.

described as 'of a more luxurious type than those normally found'. Inside the turret the adjutant/machine gunner's seat was fitted in the centre above the propshaft casing, the commander's as usual under the cupola and the second radio operator had his mounted diagonally in the rear right corner. Of course it is entirely possible that individual commanders had their tanks modified to suit their own preferences – for example, some tanks had metal ladders or steps added to the trackguards to make mounting and dismounting easier.

Panzerbeobachtungswagen (Artillery observation tank)

The SdKfz 143 *Artillerie Panzerbeobachtungswagen* III was a converted Panzer III (from Ausf E onwards) used by artillery observation officers to locate targets and control the fire from the supporting self-propelled gun batteries. It had a four-man crew and for self-defence an MG34 was mounted in a ball mount in the centre of

ABOVE The SdKfz 143 *Artillerie Panzerbeobachtungswagen* III. This had a distinctive mantlet with the MG34 defence weapon in the centre and the dummy 37mm alongside. The studs for mounting the additional flush-fitting 30mm plates on the hull front are clearly visible. (TM 2361/E2)

BELOW The FuG 8 radio used by artillery observation officers as well as being the main divisional command radio – this was the same set that used the *Rahmenantenne* or *Sternantenne* on the *Befehlswagen*. (Courtesy Malteserfunk)

BELOW The *Tornister Funkgerät* b (Torn.Fu.b) backpack radio.

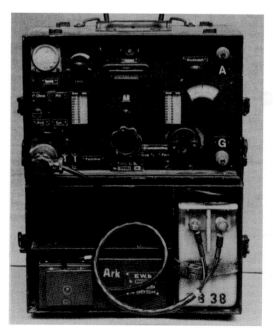

ABOVE A camouflaged *Panzerbeobachtungswagen*. *(TM 2362/A1)*

BELOW This *Panzerbeobachtungswagen* has a different style of front armour to others seen, but the square opening in the mantlet centre is distinctive of the type. Note also the antenna base on the engine decks. *(TM 2361/E4)*

BELOW *Flammpanzer* III – this tank was captured by the British in Italy where a number were deployed. Note the thickness of the dummy barrel and the late hull without escape hatches. The turret number is indistinct but starts with an F.

the turret, with a tubular stub to the left of it to allow a pipe representing a 37mm gun barrel to be fitted; armour was increased to 30mm all-round. It carried two role-specific radios. The FuG 8 was a 30W medium-wave transmitter/receiver which used a *Sternantenne*, whereas the FuG 4, also MW, could only receive. A backpack radio (probably one of the *Tornister Funkgerät* series aka *Torn.Fu.*) was also carried for use away from the vehicle, but the most interesting piece of radio equipment carried was probably the *Funksprechgerät* (radio speaker apparatus). This transmitted over distance to loudspeakers mounted on the self-propelled guns (*Wespe* or *Hummel*), allowing them to hear the orders of the artillery observation officer and his corrections of fire. Some 268 tanks were recorded as being so converted, 225 during 1943 and the remainder in the first four months of 1944. Two were allocated to each *Hummel* or *Wespe* battery.

Flammpanzer (Flamethrower)

In 1940, 43 Panzer II light tanks were ordered to be converted to flamethrower tanks (*Flammpanzer*) in light of experience gained in the early campaigns. These tanks had additional small turrets mounted on the front for the flame-guns, and fuel was externally stored on the trackguards, not the most obvious place. Although they only had an effective range of about 30m and were too thinly armoured to be used in street fighting, they must have been broadly successful and proved the concept as it was later decided to convert the Panzer III to the role, it being a larger and more modern tank with better mobility and protection, as well as ensuring maximum standardisation of spare parts. This was called the SdKfz 141/3, or *Flammpanzer* III.

One hundred Ausf Ms were supplied (without main armament) by MIAG to Wegmann of Kassel for conversion to *Flammpanzer*s between February and April 1943. In place of the normal main gun a flame projector designed by a certain Herr Bode was fitted, with the MG34 retained as a coaxial weapon for close defence. Welded steel fuel tanks containing fuel oil were fitted on the floor, either side of the propeller shaft, and connected by a pipe; these were below the level of the turret ring to allow for traverse and to give maximum protection. The fuel was described as petrol thickened with tar, which gave it a distinctive smell similar to creosote. Fuel transfer into these tanks was by means of a portable hand-operated rotary pump, carried inside the vehicle. A DKW 28hp engine and pump was mounted on the left side of the fighting compartment, capable of delivering around 7 litres per second from the tanks to the projector. The 2in fuel piping used inside the turret was of the flexible, wire-bound type. The weapon was mounted inside a tubular steel casing welded to the inside of the mantlet, with two *Smits* spark plugs, a weighted counterbalance and a pressure gauge on the rear. It was fired using a foot-operated pedal (left for MG, right for flame), with traverse and elevation controlled by handwheels to the left front of the commander. Sighting was by means of a simple rear- and fore-sight on the cupola and mantlet sleeve respectively. Additional fire extinguishers were – sensibly – carried.

The crew was reduced to three – the driver and radio operator/hull machine gunner, plus the commander who also operated the flame gun.

LEFT Kharkov, 1943 – from the thickness of the barrel and the aiming post mounted to the mantlet, this appears to be a *Flammpanzer*.

Unlike British versions (*eg* Churchill Crocodile) all the fuel was contained within the hull and it did not need to tow a conspicuous trailer. In order to camouflage the role of the tank, the stubby flame gun was surrounded by a long metal tube, resembling a large-calibre tank barrel and about 1.5m long with a diameter of 120mm. Due to the short range of the weapon, only about 50m, an

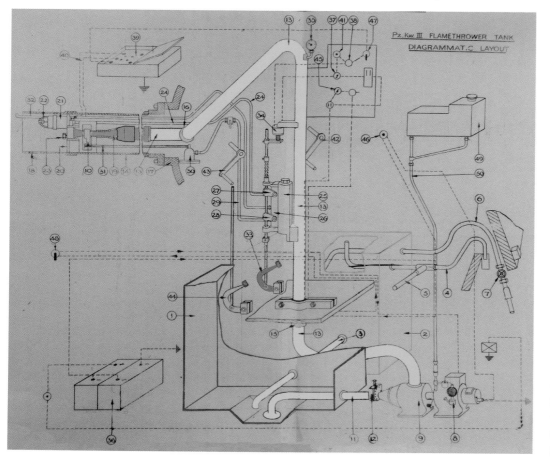

LEFT A British diagram showing the installation within the turret of a *Flammpanzer* III. The two fuel tanks (sectionalised) are in red (left) and orange (right), the main fuel pipe in yellow, the 14mm nozzle in green and the firing pedal in blue.

RIGHT A Momsen
apparatus being
used by an American
sailor. Similar devices
were used on the
Tauchpanzer.
(US Navy)

additional 30mm of appliqué armour was fitted to
the nose plate. The intention was to allocate seven
of the tanks of the staff company of each panzer
regiment, and some units were issued them in
mid-1943. When they were no longer required, a
number were reported as being converted (back)
to gun tanks, with others to StuG III.

Tauchpanzer (Diving tank)

Tauchpanzer was the name given to a number
of tanks converted for deep snorkelling in

preparation for Operation *Seelöwe* (Sealion) –
the invasion of Britain.[16] The tank was sealed
(a task helped enormously by the use of
welding rather than riveting) with all hatches and
openings closed off used rubber sheeting and
sealant (cable tar). A 20cm wire-bound rubber
snorkel tube to obtain air was designed to float
above the surface of the water, with the exhaust
pipes extended and non-return valves fitted to
prevent water ingress; a bilge pump was fitted
to discharge leakage. The large open area at
the hull rear under-hang was sealed using large
flaps welded in place. It was estimated that
a trained crew would take about 24 hours to
complete the preparations for submersion.

Around September and October 1940
a group of soldiers from Pz Regt 2 were
used to form *Panzer Abteilung* A and began
training with the new machines; later two
other battalions, B and C, were formed. The
crews were all volunteers, and it was just as
well as the work was hazardous. Although
US-designed Momsen rebreather apparatus
was issued, at least 20 tank crewmen drowned
during the trials.

Although they were never used against
Britain, *Tauchpanzer* did see service during
Operation Barbarossa, including the crossings
of the rivers Bug and Dnieper by 18 Pz Regt
in the 18th Pz Div. In July 1941, while crossing

16 The invasion was more bluff than reality; although preparations were
made, these were intended to convince Britain to come to terms.

BELOW *Tauchpanzer* in action – the tanks were launched on to the bottom
of the sea from a lighter with a ramp. The depth of the water should be
15m maximum, as the tubes were 18m long to give a margin of safety.
Underwater direction was kept using the gyrocompass and the buoyancy of
the tanks made steering on the seabed quite easy.

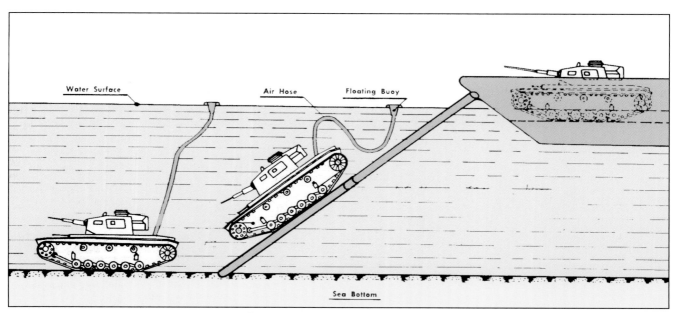

the latter, a problem was reported that would not have occurred during Operation Sealion. Enemy fire was damaging the sealing, as the tanks were of necessity having to enter the water within the range of enemy guns, and not surprisingly attracted a lot of their attention.

A British intelligence report from August 1945 commented on a different design, probably a one-off. This was a turretless Panzer III used for deep wading on a seaplane base

ABOVE LEFT AND ABOVE *Tauchpanzer*: a number of tank crewmen were drowned during sea trials – escaping from the driver's position could only be undertaken via the turret, an almost impossible task.

RIGHT *Putlos*: interested officers inspect a prepared Panzer III Ausf E with the rubber air intake and exhaust tubes folded along the hull; note the signal port cover on the turret roof. The turret side hatch is open – one must hope that it was correctly sealed before use.

LEFT Deep fording rather than swimming – a command tank emerges from a river crossing. Because it has a non-traversing turret, extra track links are carried above the hull front, and note the wooden logs carried on the engine decks, which were used to assist in crossing muddy areas. *(TM 3538/A1)*

RIGHT The
Munitionspanzer III
with the cover
elevated and propped
up. Note the short
sections of *Schürzen*
with vision slots cut in
the top. *(TM 1910/C3)*

on Sylt Island west of Flensburg. It was not designed for prolonged submersion, but rather just enough to allow it to complete its job: it appeared to have been used to tow a trailer into the water to allow a boat to be floated from it. A hemispherical Perspex cupola 20in in diameter was mounted on the hull roof, and was described as being marked in mils in the inside which was intriguingly described as being 'similar to those used on explosive motorboats'. All hatches were waterproofed using rubber strips, and an engine air intake pipe about 8ft tall was mounted on to a bracket at the rear of the engine compartment. A 4ft 7in wide towing bracket made out of 8in channel iron was fitted across the rear of the hull.

RIGHT Ammunition
transfer from a
Munitionspanzer. The
canvas cover appears
to have been folded
back over the engine
decks.

Munitionspanzer III

Once the Panzer III was supplanted by the Panzer IV with its long 75mm gun, redundant chassis were employed in a number of roles. One of these involved conversion into an ammunition carrying tank, or *Munitionspanzer*. The turret was removed, along with the components related to its previous role as a gun tank – ammunition lockers, rotating base junction, stowage, etc. New ammunition containers were built inside the hull to carry the maximum number of shells for the tanks that they were supporting, and were probably specific for each type of ammunition. For crew (and ammunition) protection from the elements, a circular canvas cover was fitted over a round wire framework. The new vehicle, being so much lighter than a gun tank with turret, must have been quite a manoeuvrable beast.

Bergepanzer (Recovery tank)

In January 1944 it was decided, in typical German fashion, that the hulls of obsolete Panzer III gun tanks should be converted into recovery tanks, known as *Bergepanzer* III. The idea was possibly inspired by units removing unserviceable turrets from gun tanks and using them in this role, albeit without any specialist recovery equipment fitted – although

6 Panzer Division at Kursk were clearly an enterprising formation as they fitted a large crane to one hull. Turrets and other internal fittings were removed, the crew being given a wooden box superstructure to provide them with some form of protection from the weather, if not the enemy. In the course of conversion at least some had the *Zimmerit* anti-mine coating applied, and the new *Ostketten* tracks were usually fitted.[17] Mounting blocks for fitting a 2-ton jib crane were welded to the superstructure on the left side, and a large earth anchor was devised to give the tank purchase when recovering heavy equipment. In total about 262 were converted; in March 1945 130 were still listed as operational.

The Panzer III/IV *mit Schachtellaufwerk*

The intention with this vehicle was to produce a standardised tank that used the best features of both Panzers III and IV, plus some novel technology (in the form of the suspension), in order to field a single medium tank and

---

17 It is tempting to wonder if Herr Zimmer of Rheinmetall had a hand in its invention.

LEFT The distinctive wooden box structure of a *Bergepanzer*. Note the extended tracks, developed to cope with the muddy conditions in Russia. *(TM 2361/E5)*

BELOW An abandoned *Bergepanzer* complete with *Zimmerit*, probably in Germany, early 1945. A turretless engineer variant was also made, as were Panzer IIIs used as mine-clearing vehicles or modified to operate on railway tracks. *(TM 2362/A5)*

ABOVE Mud trials; note the early hull features. The new suspension had to be severely tested in such conditions as mud packing between the wheels was known to be a problem. *(TM 53/E4 and E5)*

it was known that weight distribution was more even than with other systems, but the problem was once again mud, which tended to pack between the wheels and caused many failures. Based on the hull of the Ausf H, it was to carry more armour than previously, with 50mm all round for the battle tank variant and 40mm on the sides and rear of the fire support tank. One intention was to base the turret upon the Panzer IV with its larger turret ring, and this was to feature hydraulic power traverse (although traverse would be limited to only 135° either side of gun front to simplify manufacture). If successful, the plan would have been to bring the tank into production by the end of 1944, but it was finally cancelled just before that in favour of larger, more modern designs. Herr Kniepkamp, the technical chief in *Waffenamt Prüfwesen* 6 (*Wa Prüf* 6), was responsible for AFV (armoured fighting vehicle) development and who had been the driving force behind advancing the successful Ausf E with its more powerful engine, higher speed, thicker armour and torsion bar suspension. He strongly believed that the Panzer III/IV design should have been adapted to replace both the III and IV, making the larger and more complicated Panthers and Tigers unnecessary, and which could have been produced in very large numbers. He was overruled by the likes of Speer, who wanted ever larger and heavier tanks with which to dominate the battlefield.

simplify production. A note from September 1941 described the perceived advantages that would come from such a design; these included less demand on draughtsmen, a reduced requirement for testing, less experimental vehicles, standardisation of all parts except for the armament and related components (ammunition stowage, sights, etc.), increased ammunition stowage over the existing Panzer III and the ability to switch production between the different armaments to meet demand.

Interleaved roadwheels were favoured by FAMO, the suspension designers, because

RIGHT The experimental Panzer III/IV with the FAMO-designed suspension. *(TM 617/B1)*

Miscellaneous variants

RIGHT The Russians captured many Panzer IIIs and StuG IIIs, and turned the chassis of some into this beast, called the SU76i – the i stood for *inostrannaya* (foreigner). Converted in Factory No 38 at Kirov, it mounted the standard Soviet 76.2mm ZIS-3 or S-1 gun in a fixed superstructure and between 200 and 600 were built, some as command vehicles. A number were used at Kursk in July 1943, and one example was reported as being recaptured by the Germans in early 1944, and used by *Pz Jg Abt* 128.

LEFT This Panzer III (or possibly StuG III) has had its *bugpanzer* superstructure removed and is being used by US troops to assist in a railway marshalling yard; it appears to have had a towing hook added to the rear. *(TM 2362/B6)*

LEFT The StuG III was based upon the chassis of the Panzer III. This example is pictured in Russia in autumn 1943. These prolific and capable vehicles will be covered in detail in a future Haynes Manual. *(Bundesarchiv Bild 101I-087-3675A-08A)*

Chapter Three

Anatomy of the Panzer III

The Panzer III shared many features that were common with other designs, and thus can be placed into the hierarchy of development that started even before the Panzer I was conceived and ended with the Tiger II. The tank was designed around a philosophy of use that did not always prove to be useful in actual combat.

OPPOSITE A line of brand-new Panzer IIIs in *Gelb* camouflage are parked next to a sea of tracks – each set of which could take 2,000 man hours to produce.

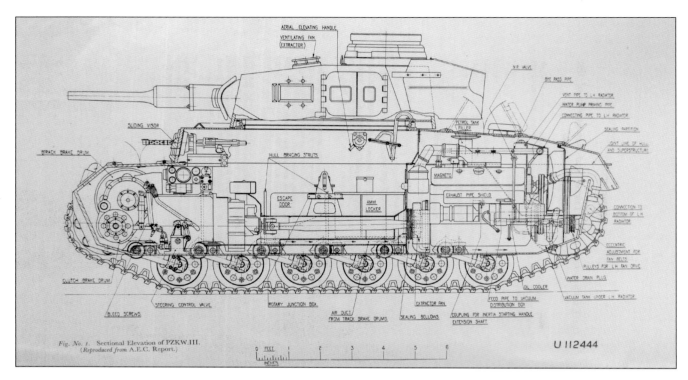

AERIAL ELEVATING HANDLE
VENTILATING FAN
(EXTRACTOR)
N.R. VALVE
BY-PASS PIPE
VENT PIPE TO L.H. RADIATOR
WATER PUMP PRIMING PIPE
CONNECTING PIPE TO L.H. RADIATOR
SLIDING VISOR
PETROL TANK FILLER
SEALING PARTITION
JOINT LINE OF HULL AND SUPERSTRUCTURE
RETRACK BRAKE DRUM
HULL BRACING STRUTS
MAGNETO
EXHAUST PIPE SHIELD
CONNECTION TO BOTTOM OF L.H. RADIATOR
ESCAPE DOOR
AMM. LOCKER
ECCENTRIC ADJUSTMENT FOR FAN BELTS
PULLEYS FOR L.H. FAN DRIVE
WATER DRAIN PLUG
OIL COOLER
VACUUM TANK UNDER L.H. RADIATOR
CLUTCH BRAKE DRUM
BLEED SCREWS
STEERING CONTROL VALVE
ROTARY JUNCTION BOX
AIR DUCT FROM TRACK BRAKE DRUMS
SEALING BELLOWS
EXTRACTOR FAN
COUPLING FOR INERTIA STARTING HANDLE EXTENSION SHAFT
FEED PIPE TO VACUUM DISTRIBUTION BOX

Fig. No. 1. Sectional Elevation of PZKW.III.
(Reproduced from A.E.C. Report.)

0 FEET 1 2 3 4 5 6
INCHES

U 112444

Introduction

As has already been explained, each model (*Ausfuhrung*) – and indeed tanks of the same model – had a variety of different characteristics and these could vary dependent on date of production, the manufacturer, modifications incorporated or as a result of field repairs. Therefore, the description here is of necessity somewhat general in nature and is intended to give an overview of a typical tank used in North Africa around 1942. It is based upon detailed observations made by a British examination of a captured tank (probably a late Ausf F), but where practical, other features pertaining to different models will be described in parallel.

Mobility

Engine and gearbox

Not surprisingly, the engine chosen for the tank was a Maybach – as were all the subsequent replacements. Pre-dating the First World War, Maybach engines were renowned for their design and build standard and had been used to power the Zeppelin airships. The engines used on the Panzer III were all petrol units with a pair of Solex Type 40 downdraught carburettors mounted between the cylinder banks. Although a Maybach design, most engines were actually made under licence by the *Norddeutsche Motorenbau* (Nordbau) in Berlin; Maybach's policy was to design and perfect an engine, and then license it for manufacture by other firms, allowing them to concentrate on the development of their next model. The basic design was extremely compact, only measuring 1210mm (L) × 814mm (W) × 880mm (H) and weighing less than 1,000kg. The first type used was the water-cooled V-12 HL108TR, an 11.95-litre unit which delivered 250hp at 2,600rpm, with maximum torque available at around 2,100rpm. When used in the early (lighter) development tanks, this gave a power-to-weight ratio of just over 17hp to the ton, a reasonably good figure.

Later the higher-powered TRM model was introduced, capable of producing 320hp but subsequently de-tuned to provide 300hp. Despite the increases in engine output, the power-to-weight ratio dropped as the tank gained armour and became heavier; by the Ausf H it was less than 13hp to the ton. The engine was mounted on a three-point rubber suspension to absorb vibration, and used a dry sump lubrication system which used 25 litres of oil. The radiators and cooling fans were

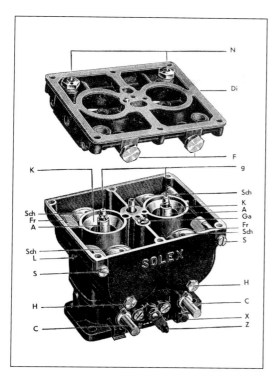

ABOVE The uprated Maybach TRM engine; most were made by Nordbau under licence.

LEFT All models used Solex carburettors.

fitted behind the engine, and a single 310-litre fuel tank was fitted on the right side, enough to give it a range of about 160km on the road, or 95km cross-country. One of a pair of 12V 105ah Varta batteries was mounted to the left-hand side. Running forward from the engine was a propeller shaft in a tunnel (this ate up a lot of valuable stowage space but was also used to pass various cables and pipes along), which was connected via a universal joint to the transmission in the centre of the nose, with the final drives bolted to the hull front on either side.

A number of different gearbox types were used as the tank developed, with *Zahnfabrik* (ZF) units manufactured in Friedrichshafen being favoured. Initially Ausf A–C used the five-speed and reverse SFG 75 unit, with a six-speed SSG 76 Aphon being adopted on the Ausf D. On the E a complicated ten-speed Maybach Variorex pre-select transmission was used, but once in use this was found to be unreliable, and was certainly a complex unit to build under increasingly difficult wartime

CENTRE AND RIGHT The extremely complicated Variorex ten-speed gearbox. The steering mechanism was integral and fitted at the front of the unit.

ABOVE AND ABOVE RIGHT The ZF Aphon gearbox, which had six forward gears plus reverse.

RIGHT The air cooling system: air was drawn in by the two large fans, entering via the side air intakes (and the raised louvres when fitted) and over the engine block, exiting out of the rear hull. From December 1941 all tanks were produced with the revised engine decks, whether *Tropen*-modified or not.

RIGHT Airflow through the vehicle. The blue arrows are the air drawn in by the bulkhead-mounted extractor fan through the front vents and over the steering brakes. Green is the turret-mounted breech ventilation fan. Red is the engine air being drawn from the turret and fighting compartment into the air cleaners. Not shown is the air cooling the engine which was drawn in by the rear-mounted fans.

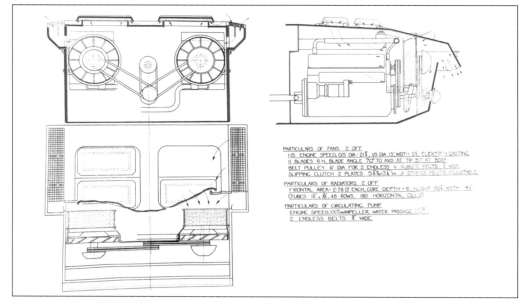

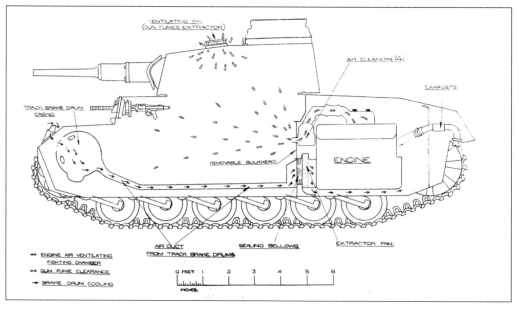

conditions; it was also used on the Panzer IV and some half-tracks. Problems with its development and manufacture contributed to the slow rate of production of the Ausf E. From the Ausf H onwards, a ZF unit was again used, this time the six forward and one reverse SSG 77 Aphon. The Aphon system mounted each gear independently on two bearings which was intended to minimise transmission noise, but it also ensured accuracy of synchromesh operation under high loads that probably led to its adoption for use on tanks.

The tank was designed to be able to climb a 30° slope and a vertical step of 600mm. It could wade about 800mm unprepared, and cross a 2.3m trench or gap.[1] In bottom gear it had a 5.9m turning circle. In its later versions the tank was claimed to have a top speed of 67kph, but this should be taken with a large pinch of salt. British trials concluded that the maximum speed (with either gearbox) on road was 25.5mph (41kph), or 21mph (34kph) cross-country. It was concluded from driving trials that sixth gear (Aphon) or eighth (Variorex) could only be used on roads, and that to all intents and purposes ninth and tenth on the latter were 'virtually useless'. Overall the Panzer III was a notably quiet tank, the engine itself being particularly so at low revs; the majority of the noise came from the gearbox and the tracks.

ABOVE The transmission shaft exposed, with four of the torsion bar pairs also visible. *(TM 6342/A1)*

Suspension

A design feature of the Panzer III which deserves some explanation is the choice of location of the gearbox, final drives, steering units and sprockets at the front of the tank. Having

LEFT Sprocket damage was a common problem, and could lead to an otherwise serviceable tank becoming non-operational. *(TM 2896/ C1 and 4868/A5)*

---

1   British tests on captured tanks stated: vertical step 2ft 0in (610mm), trench 5ft 7in (1.7 m), and fording 2ft 11in (890mm).

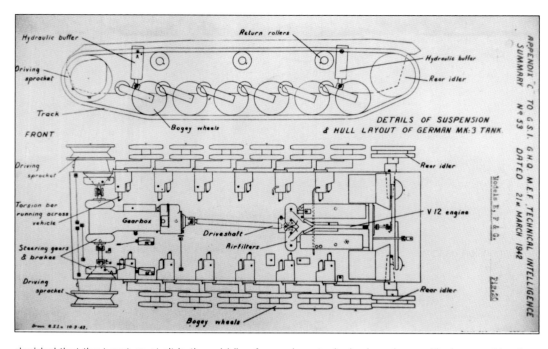

decided that the turret must sit in the middle of the hull, with the engine and fuel tank behind it, the designers had to optimise the location of other components. A great deal of thought was given as to whether to place the drive sprocket at the rear or the front, and it was concluded that there were a number of good reasons why the front was preferable. With a front drive, the tracks moving forward from the rear around the idler and over the top rollers tended to shed a lot of the mud that they would pick up, which meant less track wear and so extended track life. There was also limited space behind the engine for transmission components, and moving them forwards allowed the hull geometry to be optimised for efficient steering; it is not generally appreciated that the ratio between a tank's width and length (track on ground) greatly affects the steering characteristics and must be within certain limits otherwise the tank will either be incredibly hard to steer, or will be 'twitchy'. Another less important advantage was the short steering lines, as the driver would be co-located with the steering unit. Of course there were disadvantages too. A driveshaft would have to run forwards along the floor of the fighting compartment, taking up valuable room, and there was an increased likelihood of damage to the gearbox and drive sprocket, either from mines or enemy fire. This was certainly proved in action, as many images

show tanks broken down with damaged track and sprocket.

The original five-roadwheel arrangement used on the Ausf A had proved to be unsatisfactory in trials. On the Ausf B eight pairs of small rubber-tyred roadwheels were used on either side. These were mounted in pairs on a pivoting mount, so that 1 and 2, 3 and 4, etc., were together. Each group of four were sprung by a large horizontal semi-elliptical leaf spring attached to the hull side, just above the top of the wheels. A third top roller was added behind the sprocket. On the Ausf C the roadwheel arrangements were the same as the B, but the first and last pairs had their own smaller leaf spring, with a third larger one in the centre of the hull for the middle four wheels. This design showed promise, so on the Ausf D the general arrangement was retained but with the front and rear small springs set at a shallow angle, rather than horizontally; this was probably to account for the extra movement required of the first and last roadwheels when crossing obstacles. The gearbox was also changed to a six-speed version. The early development suspensions used on the Ausf A–D all shared one common feature – they were complex and used a lot of external components. This meant that they were susceptible to damage in action and collected a lot of mud even when not. As well as this, the trials crews believed (correctly)

RIGHT The first type of vertical shock absorber used, with a distinctive corrugated gaiter on the top. No doubt due to difficulties in obtaining materials, it was made of leather rather than rubber. This proved susceptible to damage and was replaced by an all-metal version.

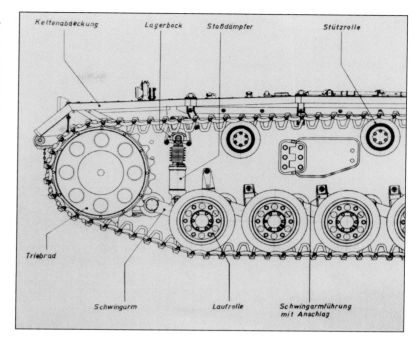

Kettenabdeckung   Lagerbock   Stoßdämpfer   Stützrolle

Triebrad

Schwingarm   Laufrolle   Schwingarmführung mit Anschlag

that it could be improved to give a better ride cross-country – after all was said and done, the Panzer III was meant to have manoeuvrability as its primary characteristic. The designers worked hard to produce a better solution, and when the Ausf E came into production in December 1938 the suspension used was the one employed, with minor modifications, for the rest of the life of the tank.

Torsion bar suspensions are commonly used now, but in the 1930s it was quite a revolutionary concept. Its adoption on German tanks including the Panzer III is generally attributed to the 'genius' of Ferdinand Porsche. However, it is now known that he adopted – or plagiarised – the idea after becoming aware of the work of Hans Ledwinka, an Austrian working for Tatra in Czechoslovakia who specialised in suspension systems. When a roadwheel encounters uneven ground it needs to move up and down, and as much as possible of the forces transmitted to it should be prevented from being transmitted in turn to the hull and the crew. Therefore the suspension has two requirements: to absorb the shock by some form of spring, and then to damp the oscillations quickly to return the spring back to its resting state, otherwise the suspension will cause the vehicle to bounce. A torsion bar does this by using a long bar of

LEFT The Luvax shock absorbers were fitted only to the first and last roadwheels, these being the ones which experienced the most force and movement when crossing obstacles. Lack of the correct fluid led to many of them failing in use, another example of the supply problems faced by the tank crews throughout the war.

FAR LEFT AND LEFT The trailing arms were connected to the free ends of the torsion bars, with a stub axle on which to mount the roadwheels. Upward movement of the axle was limited by a rubber stop.

ABOVE Torsion bars were sometimes carried in this manner, indicating that they were prone to failing and required immediate changing in the field.

BELOW The main hull plates: Section XX (red line) shows the intrusion of the torsion bars (green) into the fighting compartment, and the yellow items are the hull-stiffening members with the engine bulkhead behind.

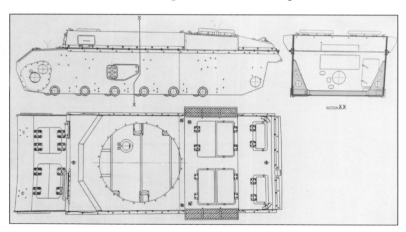

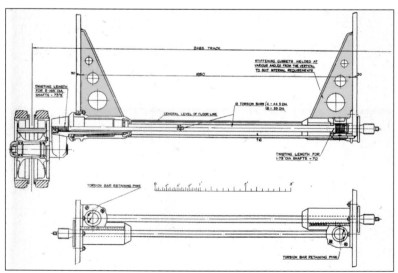

treated steel that runs transversely across the bottom of the vehicle hull. It is fixed at the end opposite the wheel it works with. The wheel axle is fitted to the bar, such that when moving up and down the bar itself twists in response to the motion of the wheel. Resistance to this twisting force provides the shock absorption function, and the tendency of the bar to want to return to its resting, untwisted state, provides the damping. The system is simple with few external components, but does take up some of the scarce internal volume at the bottom of the hull, and can be time-consuming to change if the torsion bar breaks or cracks. When it was introduced on to the Panzer III it was still not perfect, and additional hydraulic piston shock absorption with damping was found to be necessary; this issue plus problems with the gearbox and tracks put back the production of Ausf E by over a year.

A false floor about 90mm deep covered the area occupied by the torsion bars. One of the by-products of using torsion bar suspension is that the roadwheels on each side are offset in regard to their opposite number; on the Panzer III those on the right side were about 125mm further forward than those on the left. (A comparison of the gap between the rear roadwheel and the sprocket on both sides will demonstrate this.) On Panzer III the torsion bars were designed to twist 26° in order to absorb shock, before overcoming the resistance and returning to the (untwisted) resting state, returning the trailing axle and wheel with it. Initially, the front and rear torsion bars were slightly thicker and therefore stiffer than the remainder, in order to support the additional weight of the gun and armour above, and to prevent pitching; this of course complicated supply, as at least three thicknesses of bar were employed, and the designers constantly altered the thickness of the bars in an attempt to find the optimum solution. The roadwheels had an overall diameter of 520mm and were fitted with rubber tyres usually made by either Continental

LEFT The torsion bar system: pins were used to secure the end opposite the swing arm axle. The level of the floorplate above the bars is shown as the red line.

ABOVE Roadwheels came in different widths and were made with a ribbed steel rim, designed to allow damaged rubber tyres to be replaced.

LEFT AND BELOW
The top roller wheels rotated on a stub axle protruding from a conical mounting, which fitted on to three threaded studs on the hull sides.

or Vorwerk; the steel rim diameter was 392mm. To limit the upwards movement of the 225mm trailing stub axles, rubber bump stops were fitted to the middle four wheel stations which prevented the trailing arms from moving too far up and over-stressing the bars – these of course were the stations without independent shock absorbers. Once this new suspension system was adopted, the space created meant that escape hatches could also be fitted either side of the hull, allowing egress from the fighting compartment, although on some captured tanks examined in North Africa it was noted that stowed ammunition often blocked these on the inside. Overall and when compared to their in-service Crusader tank with Christie suspension, British experts considered the German suspension system to be better; it gave a similar ride but used fewer parts and weighed less, and was better protected as well.

On all types the 750mm rear idler was mounted on to a stub axle, which was adjustable to allow the crew to take up track tension when they became slack; photographs show that most crews kept the tracks almost bow-string tight, as slack tracks required more steering effort and were more prone to being shed on bad ground or when turning. The tensioning device was a large bell crank lever engaged with the idler wheel, and this was tightened (rotating the idler wheel upwards and rearwards) using a large spanner. The front sprockets (850mm tooth to opposing tooth) had 21 teeth which meshed into slots on the outsides of the tracks; these featured central guide horns that kept the track centralised. The

tracks began as 360mm wide, but even before the experiences in North Africa and Russia wider (380mm and then 400mm) tracks began to be used.[2] A wider track was developed in 1942 because of the terrible mud, snow and ice encountered in Russia; these were known

2   It was noted in North Africa that three different widths of roadwheel were in use, presumably to be used with the different tracks. If a roadwheel was fitted that was wider than the track, the rubber tyre would rapidly become badly damaged.

LEFT AND BELOW
Tracks with the track pin – note the retaining collar at one end of the pin and the hole through the opposite side which was for an S-shaped retaining device.

ABOVE Track maintenance in the field; the tank appears to be a brand new Ausf L, so this is probably a posed photograph.

Electrical components

Two 12V batteries were mounted, one in a metal container on the left-hand side of the floor of the fighting compartment and the other on the left side of the engine. This was poor design, as when charging, the temperatures of each unit would be different (the one in the engine much hotter) and the resultant difference in internal resistance would lead to unequal charging. Electrical power for the turret was passed from a rotary base junction on the hull floor via cables running up the frame of the gunner's seat, into the turret wiring loom. The purpose of the rotary base junction was to pass electrical power between the hull and turret (including radio circuits) while allowing the turret complete freedom of traverse; either side of it were two footplates for the commander's use. A number of different external lights were fitted to the tank, both front and rear. A pair of headlamps were mounted, one on either extremity of the sloping front plate, outboard of the brake air inlets. Mounted on the extremities of the front trackguards were the smaller sidelights. Alongside the left-hand sidelight was a Notek (a contraction of the Nova Technik company of Munich) tactical driving light; this had a flat-topped shield to prevent the light being seen from the air and could be used as the solitary front light when moving tactically at night, when a dim pool of light illuminated the area immediately in front, but which was not visible over large distances.

Fitted to the rear left was a Notek combined tail and convoy light. This had a hinged flap which could be used to cover the lower tail lamps leaving only four small square green (sometimes red) glass windows exposed.

as *Winterketten* (winter tracks) and used the standard track pins, but protruded outwards – past the trackguards – from the tank.[3] They began to be used from October 1942. Rubber-tyred 310mm top rollers (on 203mm rims) were fitted on to conical mounts with a simple stub axle, bolted to the hull side walls.

---

3   A report noted that as an expedient measure in 1941 in Russia, heavy wooden extensions were bolted on, but not surprisingly these did not work.

RIGHT The Notek *tarnscheinwerfer* tactical driving light. The hood shielded the light from above and also cast a dimmable pool of light in front of the tank.

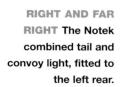

RIGHT AND FAR RIGHT The Notek combined tail and convoy light, fitted to the left rear.

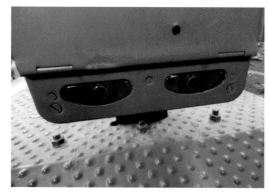

This was used as a station-keeping device to maintain the correct distance in a convoy. At the correct distance of 25m, the following driver would be able to make out two of the green lights. Too close and all four could be seen, and too far apart and all he would see was a green stripe. Lifting the hinged flap exposed two red rectangular or crescent-shaped tail lamps. A separate circular single tail lamp with red filters was fitted on the opposite (right) side. The driver controlled the illumination of the tactical driving light (front) and the tail/convoy light (rear) from a switch on the instrument panel, with the following five combinations: both off; front only on; both on with front dim; both on with front medium; and both on with front bright.

The driver's instrument panel was mounted above the gearbox to the driver's right, and incorporated: a large rev counter; speedometer; oil pressure gauge; water temperature gauge; horn button; starter button; and light switches and fuses. An electric gyrocompass called the *Anschütz Kurskreisel* was sometimes fitted to the front left of the driver. This had two dials; the upper one was the 'control dial' and was set by the driver to correspond to the desired course (heading), and the lower one was the 'following dial', which responded to the gyros to show the actual course being taken. The petrol gauge was not to be found on the instrument panel, but was mounted in the fighting compartment on the engine bulkhead at floor level, with a two-position switch above it used to turn the fuel supply on or off and to operate the fuel drain tap. The battery master switch was also mounted on the bulkhead.

The radio operator was provided with up to two radio receivers, mounted side by side over the gearbox to his left, and one transmitter,

LEFT The tail light mounted to the right rear.

mounted to his front below the roof of the glacis plate. Externally mounted on the right rear of the hull superstructure was a single rod antenna, noticeably thicker than the British equivalent; it measured 2m long and was made of copper. It had a diameter of 29mm at the base, tapering to only 4mm at the top. This could be raised or lowered from within the fighting compartment and rested in a wooden trough when not in use.

BELOW The driver's instrument panel. The tachometer red-lined from 2,800 to 3,200rpm, and the speedometer was optimistically marked up to 100kph.

FAR LEFT AND LEFT The *Kurskreisel* gyrocompass. The large knob under the window was either red or yellow, and the scale was dark grey over yellow. On the right are the binocular eyepieces used by the driver when his armoured visor was closed in action.

It was designed so that it would be temporarily depressed if the main gun or turret rear bin traversed on to it, with leaf springs causing it to reassert once the obstruction had moved out of the way.[4] Some of the crew also had a form of intercommunication for use within the tank. The commander and radio operator both used headphones plus carbon-granule throat microphones for talking on the radio or to each other, the driver only had headphones, and the other two had nothing. Strangely, from the point of view of standardisation, two different models of headphones and throat microphones were in use on the tank and which were not interchangeable. British experts thought that the radio system and technology was inferior, with low levels of resonance in the high frequencies making intelligibility of the spoken word difficult, particularly when there was a lot of background noise.

A simple rubber speaking tube from the commander to the gunner was sometimes fitted. Harness junction boxes were provided for the commander and radio operator; these had a switch marked *BORD* (intercom) and *FUNK* (radio). They also featured a call button, an indicator lamp, and separate sockets for the headset and microphone. The driver's box was simpler, only having the headphone sockets and call button. The standard radio used was the FuG 5,[5] which comprised a

ABOVE The headphones used by the commander looked identical to, but were in fact slightly different from, the ones used by the other crew members so they were not interchangeable. This Ausf N has turret *Schürzen* plates fitted. *(Bundesarchiv)*

4 From mid-1941 the turret bin had wooden strips fitted to insulate it when it came into contact with the aerial.
5 Sometimes the shorter abbreviation Fu was used, thus Fu 5.

ABOVE The FuG 5: receiver on the left, transmitter on the right. On the Panzer III these would be mounted separately, not alongside each other.

LEFT A complete FuG 5 installation with the power supply units on top; on the Panzer III one or two of the receivers (left) were mounted to the left of the operator above the transmission, and a single transmitter (right) was mounted under the glacis in front of him.

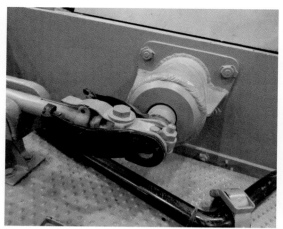

10W S.c transmitter linked to a separate Ukw Ee receiver. It operated in the VHF range, from 27.2 to 33.3MHz. On a mobile tank, the maximum range expected from it was around 4km using voice; when static, Morse could be sent about twice that distance. When a Ukw Ee receiver was fitted with no transmitter, it was referred to as a FuG 2. Company and platoon commanders' tanks were fitted with both a FuG 5 and a separate FuG 2, whereas normal platoon gun tanks only had a FuG 5.

Operating the FuG 5 radio equipment

These instructions come from the German user handbook:

Before using the equipment, check that all the connections are correctly made: the power leads for the receiver and transmitter must not be interchanged, and the headset and throat microphone connections look similar but must be fitted into the correct sockets. Adjust the set to the required frequency – instructions for each unit are on the inside of the protective lid, which is stowed above the unit when not in use. If the range to the other (receiving) radio set is less than 200m away, set the range switch to Near (Short Range). Otherwise, select Far (Long Range). Switch the volume control to low volume, and then adjust the tuning control to obtain the loudest volume. Set the volume control to the required volume for use. Periodically use the tuning control to check that the set remains on frequency.

ABOVE The internal aerial raising and lowering mechanism, and the external mechanism with leaf springs.

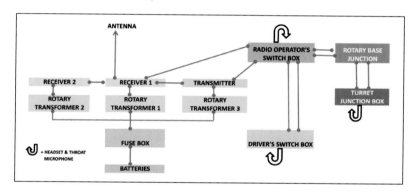

To shut the set down, switch the volume control to off and rotate the antenna into the stowed position.

ABOVE A schematic diagram of the main radio components in the Panzer III.

Automotive reliability

In the course of a 120km route march conducted in January 1940, of the 12 Panzer IIIs taking part, four broke down requiring workshop attention, and another had to be written off; presumably it either caught fire or suffered irreparable damage after coming off the road. Although the terrain was mountainous and therefore difficult, a breakdown rate of 42% per 120km on a training exercise is not an indication of a reliable tank. When Panzer Regiment 1 was training for future operations in spring 1940 it received its first Ausf E and F tanks fitted with the new Variorex gearbox. These proved to be very unreliable, as did the torsion bars fitted to wheel number one, which often broke. Frequently the transmission problems, attributed to poor design and manufacture, were serious enough

ABOVE Real
maintenance taking
place on a Panzer III
with the early-war
suspension.

BELOW Spare track
pins were often carried
in large numbers,
either stuck through
the grills on the air
intakes or behind the
appliqué armour on
the driver's visor.
(TM 18/B1)

for the whole tank to require extensive workshop repairs, and a lack of spare parts meant that sometimes a repair could only be conducted after a replacement part had been specially made. These and other automotive problems severely restricted tactical training. In October 1941 the *Panzertruppenschule* in Wunstorf admitted that 'at first the Panzer III broke down frequently', with steering and gearbox problems high on the list. One of the other reasons for this automotive unreliability was found to be dirty fuel pipes, which were easily fixed but caused inconvenient short-term breakdowns.

Overall, the Maybach engine was assessed as being easy to strip and assemble, and in general terms the build standard was high; following repairs they were able to be run-up outside the tank on a test-bed stand. One

of the many captured German documents from North Africa subsequently translated for intelligence value spoke of 'excessive trouble due to bogie [roadwheel] tyre failures, and engine failures due to sand passing the air cleaners'. It went on to explain that 'sand blocked oil supply pipes, causing wreckage of the crankshaft and pistons, and also sand in the distributor, dynamo and starter … the air filters were entirely inadequate'.

The steel roadwheel rims were designed with the idea that if the rubber tyre failed, it could be replaced on a serviceable rim by a workshop without having to discard the whole unit. Whether or not this was actually carried out is not clear, but it seems that the method might have been in part responsible for the tendency of the tank to wreck its roadwheels. Fitting the wrong size of roadwheels for the track width also contributed, as tyres wider than the track were especially prone to damage. As a British report noted, 'Bogie[6] tyre failure is excessive, this is confirmed by the large number of spare bogie wheels carried.' Although not explicitly mentioned in accounts, photographs of Panzer IIIs in action sometimes show them carrying spare torsion bars, which must indicate that they were prone to damage – this led to the crews taking the spares that they most urgently and frequently needed with them. Another item often seen carried in large numbers on the Panzer III were track pins. These must have suffered from broken pins frequently, as some crews carried dozens, stowed either in the air

---

6   The British term for roadwheels.

intake louvres or behind the spaced armour of the driver's front plate.

Although generally a simple tank, sometimes the manufacturers introduced complexities into the servicing routines that the crews would have simply been unable to follow in action. For example, every four weeks they were meant to completely drain the cooling system, and then refill with a solution of clean water plus '2–3 tablespoonfuls of Henschel P.3' – whatever that was. After a few days they were then supposed to empty the system again and refill with clean water, plus anti-freeze if required. We can only wonder how many times that was actually done in an operational theatre.

Tanks built or modified for use in hot and dry conditions were annotated with a (Tp) suffix, meaning *tropen*, or tropical. Prior to this, standard tanks had been sent to North Africa with no modifications to prepare them for the conditions they would be used in. When the 5th Light Division deployed to Libya in March 1941, the workshop company of Panzer Regiment 5 recorded that 'the tanks gave little trouble, provided that they moved by night or in the cooler hours of the day, and at a fairly low speed'. This was clearly unrealistic as combat did not generally take place at night, and so the tanks would be required to be modified to ensure that they could operate in the more testing conditions of the day, leading to the belated *tropen* modification programme. This included: improving engine compartment ventilation by cutting holes in the decks and covering them with 16mm armoured cowls; increasing the radiator fan speed; adjusting the engine air intake to draw air from the turret via a flexible pipe fitted to the engine bulkhead; sealing various components against dust ingress; adding a second oil filter; and providing additional stowage for 40 litres of water (two jerrycans). Until these were implemented, the tanks continued to be badly affected by the difficult conditions: Pz Regt 5 lost 44 out of its 65 Panzer IIIs in April 1941 due to dust-induced breakdowns – 68%. Wherever the location, tanks that broke down on the march or in combat were required to identify themselves to recovery units by flying a small flag, with a black cross on a yellow rectangular background. The crews were also instructed to prepare for recovery by connecting their tow ropes to the front or rear (as appropriate), and crossing them over in readiness for the appearance of the recovery vehicle.

Driving the Panzer III

Variorex gearbox

The following instructions are taken from a British report, which used a German translation but added user experience in the form of extra advice.

Set the gearbox direction lever to neutral, the pre-selector lever to 1st gear. Depress the

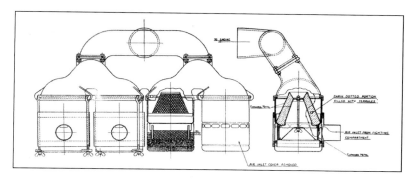

ABOVE The four oil-bath air filters mounted above the engine supplemented the original pair of element filters fitted in the bulkhead in front of the engine compartment. These in turn were replaced by Mahle filters, with air being drawn in through the turret, which reduced the amount of sand being passed into the filters.

BELOW Note the starting handle fitted into the Bosch inertial starter, and also the simple stowage rack welded to the rear hull. This tank also carries a large number of track pins in the left air intake.

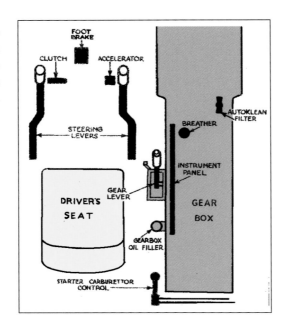

RIGHT A schematic (taken from a British report) showing the main controls in the driver's station.

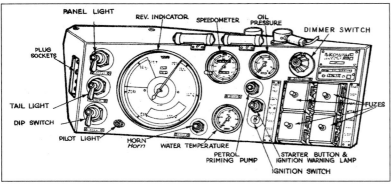

ABOVE The driver's instrument panel.

RIGHT One of the two steering units, with a rubber grip at the top. These hydraulic types were later replaced with a purely mechanical system.

clutch pedal if the engine is cold. Start the engine. (A rectangular or circular plate on the hull rear allowed the two-man starting handle to be used. This operated a geared step-up Bosch inertial starter, which could be operated from outside to engage a pinion with the flywheel, whilst the driver adjusted the throttle inside. In order to reduce the possibility of draining the tank's batteries, crews were ordered only to use the electric start method in an emergency, and never in cold weather.) Run the engine at about 1,200rpm for a few minutes to allow it to warm up so that it idles happily at 600–800rpm. Depress the clutch pedal and select forward or reverse using the gearbox direction lever. Let the clutch out slowly and the vehicle will slowly move. Set the pre-selector to the required gear; note that the gear change will not be effected until the clutch pedal is depressed and then released. As soon as the gear change is complete, set the pre-selector to the next required gear. Change up with the engine revs between 2,500–2,800rpm, and change down between 1,500–1,600rpm. Always change to a lower gear and accelerate whilst turning. When changing down during steering, on hills, and on bad roads, always change down two gears below the one in use. For the greatest fuel economy, cruise at the highest gear possible with the revs kept between 1200 and 2000. Before stopping the vehicle, select the most appropriate gear that will be used for setting off with, normally 4th. Gears 1–3 need only be used on poor going or when setting off on a slope. Note: reverse can only be used with gears 1–4.

The instructions issued to drivers make it very clear just how complicated the transmission was, with a number of specific instructions relating to gear changing in certain conditions. Without a very good understanding of how the Variorex worked, a poor driver would have had his work cut out to follow them.

Operating the ZF gearboxes was easier. First to fourth gear was as per the normal car arrangement; selecting fifth and sixth required a plunger on top of the gear change lever to be operated, allowing the lever to be moved to the right. Reverse was selected by operating a small catch in front of the gear lever, allowing it to be moved to the left and forward, which prevented inadvertent selection of reverse. It was not necessary to double declutch when changing up, and the advice was not to pause in neutral but to apply light, steady pressure to obtain the required gear. Double declutching was necessary when changing down.

Armour protection

The hull was made of a single skin of armoured steel built up by welding plates together into three sections: the hull 'tub', to which the suspension was mounted and which formed the vehicle chassis; the front superstructure (*bugpanzer*) which carried two of the crew and to which the turret race was attached; and the rear *heckpanzer*, which protected the engine and the single fuel tank. The three sub-sections were bolted together; most external bolts had a conical head and internally had a shoulder on the shank in order to reduce the risk of them being forced inside the tank if hit. In order to give the fairly thin hull tub more rigidity, additional triangular fillets were bolted across the bottom and side plates.

In the 1920s the welding of armoured plate was a huge breakthrough in the construction of tanks, which until then had been riveted. Germany was more advanced than both France and Britain, with the Krefeld-based *Deutsche Edelstahlwerke* taking the lead. Throughout the war the Hanover factory of this firm produced most of the armoured hull, superstructure and turret components, sending them to other firms located all round Germany for completion. Welding had a number of advantages over riveting. The latter required a frame on which to attach the plates, which could add as much as 4 tons to a largish tank – the rivets alone could weigh 100kg. Such a design was restricted to simple box shapes and was difficult to waterproof. Each joint between plates was a weak point, and the rivets could, if struck, become dangerous sub-projectiles, damaging systems and injuring the crew. Welding removed most of these disadvantages, as the plates themselves were self-supporting and the structure required no frame.

Although the technique of welding armour plates was a genuine breakthrough, the

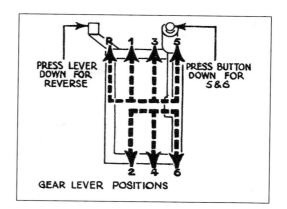

LEFT The gear gate for ZF six-speed and reverse gearboxes.

amount and quality of the welds had to be experimented with in order to give the desired strength without adding excess material or slowing down production. The German tank manufacturers do not appear to have used large manipulators to move the hulls and turrets into the right place to facilitate gravity welding, which is the most efficient type. This affected the strength of the joint, and the effects can often be seen in photographs, where Panzer IIIs that have suffered an internal explosion have been disassembled along the plate joints. And interestingly, in 1940 the Germans themselves reported that some tanks in certain climatic conditions had suffered major weld failures after only minor collisions with obstacles – a common occurrence in action. Apparently extreme cold was the real issue, making the welds brittle,

LEFT The hull side walls were thin and therefore vulnerable. Note the scalloped method of joining the hull tub to the superstructure, which was simplified on late tanks in an effort to speed up production. (TM 4868/A4)

Panzer III.

(Ray Hutchins 1988)

1 Sighting vane
2 Commander's hatch
3 Vision cupola
4 Vision block
5 MG34 coaxial machine gun
6 MG34 ammunition sacks
7 50mm main armament gun barrel
8 Gunner's vision flap
9 Maybach engine
10 Muzzle
11 Spare road wheels
12 Jack
13 50mm ammunition
14 Idler wheel
15 Shock absorber
16 Vehicle battery
17 Rotary base junction
18 Trailing arm
19 Road wheel pair
20 Driver's seat
21 Final drive
22 Steering tillers
23 Instrument panel
24 Gearbox
25 Face-hardened armour
26 Drive sprocket
27 Lifting eye
28 Track
29 Track guard
30 Radio operator's seat
31 Tool stowage
32 MG34 hull machine gun
33 MG34 head control
34 50mm recoil guard
35 Turret crew side hatch
36 50mm breech
37 Mantlet
38 Ventilation fan

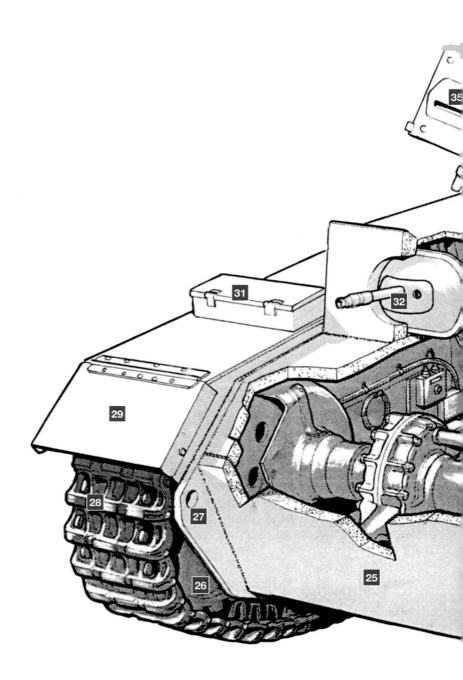

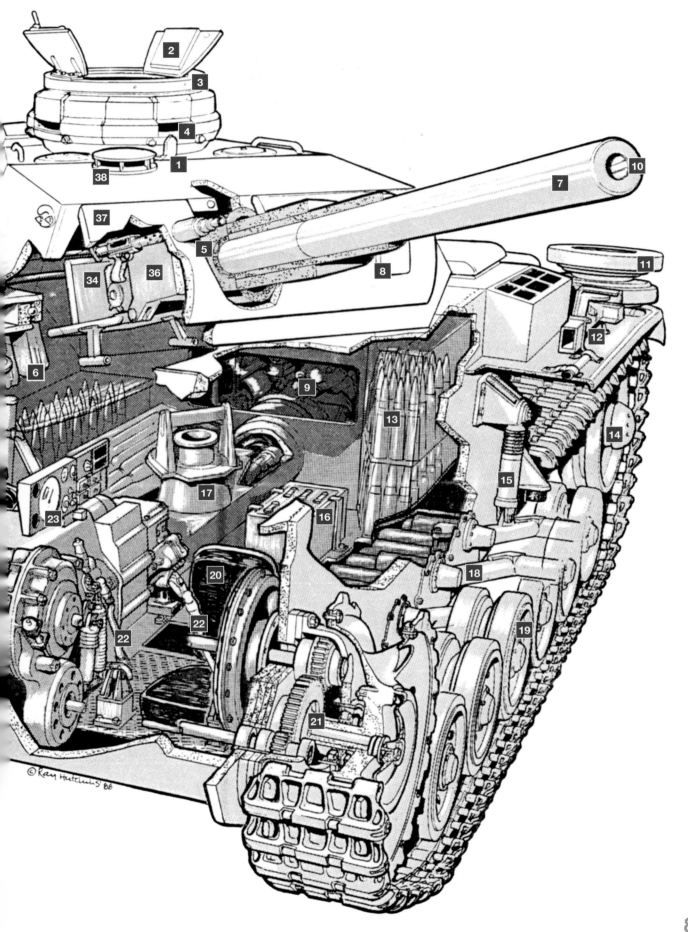

RIGHT External weld lines, here on the distinctive front turret fillet, so typical of German tanks.

BELOW A Panzer III used in British 'attack of armour' trials. Notice how the entire side and rear turret plates have been detached along the weld lines.

RIGHT This up-armoured Panzer III (note the circular *Kugelblende* MG mounting and single-piece front hatch) is in the process of being dismantled for examination; the steering brake cowls and a section of frontal armour have already been removed.
(TM 2357/E6)

which did not bode well for campaigning in the Russian winter. The Germans believed that the root cause was the ferritic electrodes being used during the welding process, and insisted in 1942 that in future only austenitic electrodes were to be employed.

British metallurgical experts from the Welding and Gas Cutting Branch were tasked to examine German welding techniques used on the Panzer III and were horrified by some of what they found. In general terms the standard of welding was often very poor, and accounted for the structural deficiencies noted above. In a lot of cases there were gaps left open, and in some instances the weld was not actually in contact with one of the two plates. One of the reasons attributed for this was the design which required each plate edge to be finely finished; where this was not done well, the lack of contact between two adjoining plates would cause the weld to be placed under too much stress, leading to fracturing. This was in stark contrast to the British view of other aspects of the tank's design and construction, where the quality of finishing was thought to be of a uniformly (and possibly in some areas unnecessarily) high standard, and brought praise from the examiners – one spoke of a 'high quality of workmanship, material and excellence of detailed design'. Whether this problem with welds was a failure of supervision (quality control) in particular factories, pressures on production, the increasing use of forced or slave labour or other factors, it is salutary to note that by 1943 the Germans, who for the previous two decades had led the world in welding armoured plate, were producing tanks with defective structures that rendered them vulnerable. This may be one of the reasons – the other being the increasing armour thicknesses – why German tank designs from the Tiger and Panther onwards adopted mortice-jointed welded armour.

Face-hardening (FH) of armour was extensively used by the Germans where the plate was expected to be hit by enemy fire, but not where the plate also had a major structural role. This is because these forces acting on a FH plate can cause the plate to deform, whereas homogeneous armour[7] resists much

---

7   Armour of the same composition and quality throughout its thickness.

better. The Germans favoured the use of FH on frontal armour because it was effective at breaking up shot on impact, particularly with the early-war, less sophisticated types of AP ammunition. From June 1940 the use of FH plate was mandated by the Weapons Office, whereas previously the manufacturers had the option of using homogeneous plate; this probably came about as a result of the experience being gained in France. Where enemy crews mentioned their ammunition 'bouncing off' German tanks, in a lot of cases what they had actually witnessed was the shot shattering on impact, and the tracer element flying into the sky.

One of the downsides of FH armour was the time it took to make; the flame-hardening processes could take up to three weeks to finish one plate, as the surface of the plate had to be repeatedly heated using oxyacetylene and then rapidly quenched in a water spray to cool. Another disadvantage was that once the hardened surface had been penetrated, the remaining armour provided much less resistance and a perforation was more likely. For example, a sample of armour tested revealed a Brinell hardness of 430 on the surface, a maximum of 570 just under the surface (⅛in), but only 335 at ¼in. This meant that once the enemy had improved the gun and/

or ammunition they were using, more armour had to be added – but if the ammunition had been specifically optimised to penetrate FH plate, the advantage was lost and the FH armour then provided less protection than if homogeneous plate had been used. This happened when 6-pounder APCBC (armour-piercing capped ballistic cap) ammunition was introduced in 1943, as a combination of the cap on the ammunition and the strike energy of the projectile meant that the Panzer III could be penetrated with relative ease. An Ausf J was used as the target in British firing trials in May 1943; the report concluded that 'armour protection against 2-pounder AP is good, but

LEFT A destroyed Panzer III *lang* in North Africa – the explosion has separated the superstructure from the hull, but the turret has remained attached. *(TM 2896/D2)*

RIGHT Ammunition stowage for the main gun varied, but most of the ammunition was stowed in steel storage lockers positioned in the rear corners of the fighting compartment. Not all were readily available to the loader.

RIGHT AND BELOW The 20mm *Vorpanzer* or appliqué plate in front of the existing 30mm protecting the driver's and radio operator's positions; it was fitted using simple brackets welded to the superstructure, and gave a 100mm stand-off. The space between was often used by crews as a stowage area for spare track pins, and the blue fillers shown in the diagram were not always seen on service tanks.

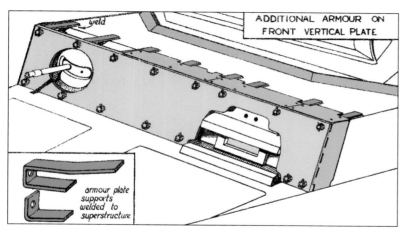

protection against 6-pounder AP is poor'. The strike energy of the 6-pounder, even when it failed to penetrate, frequently broke open the weld seams along their entire length. Other British tests conducted on captured tanks also found that the appliqué armour plates were harder than the actual tank armour; whereas the 50mm front armour (on an Ausf J) had a surface Brinell hardness of around 550, the 30mm appliqué in front of it was 750. This may indicate a deliberate policy of trying to use the appliqué to break up uncapped shot; equally it might just reflect poor quality control and inconsistency during manufacture. Welding of FH armour was practicable, but had the undesired effect of reducing the protection locally (where heat had been applied), again making the welds and the areas immediately surrounding them weaker than the main armour plates. If an engineer wished to destroy a Panzer III completely, packing plastic explosive inside the welded joints would be an economical method, almost guaranteed to tear the tank apart along the seams.

German ammunition was well protected within the tanks, being stowed in steel bins about 5mm thick and kept as low in the hull as possible. A German report from Poland (where anti-tank defences were less capable than in later campaigns) stated that only one in five hits resulted in a penetration of the armour, and this usually resulted in only one crew member being killed or injured, with the driver and radio operator the most likely to become casualties. Later reports from North Africa made it clear that the Panzer III, even when penetrated, remained a difficult vehicle to destroy. Penetrations could result in crew injuries or deaths, but the tank itself frequently remained in action or at least was readily repairable; one report estimated that only around 20% of German tanks knocked out in North Africa were unable to be repaired. This was a tribute to sensible design, as vehicle fires were mainly caused by stowed ammunition being detonated, rather than by fuel (as was commonly assumed at the time). Using *benzin* (petrol) as the fuel was therefore not a mistake as some commentators have believed. Interestingly, the choice of using petrol in their tanks was a conscious decision made by the

Germans pre-war. They rightly believed that they would become reliant on synthetic fuel, and producing synthetic petrol was assessed to be much easier than making diesel.

The addition of various thicknesses of appliqué armour, known as *Zusatzpanzerung* (additional armouring) was a simple and effective means of increasing the inadequate protection of the original 30mm front hull plate. As previously mentioned, German design philosophy was that the frontal aspect of the tank was deemed to be the most likely area to be hit, and so any additional armour had to be fitted there. This was technically incorrect as it failed to recognise the high likelihood of being hit on the sides, particularly as ever-more intelligent enemies were seeking to exploit known weaknesses; the thin side armour of the Panzer III was no exception (and which belatedly led to additional measures being introduced in 1943, see below). One of the great advantages of appliqué armour systems are that they are simple to introduce without disturbing production, and can be applied to vehicles already in the field. Care has to be taken not to interfere with existing systems, and in some cases new components, particularly the driver's vision visor and the bow MG mounting, had to be designed, but this was not a major problem. In some cases the extra armour was bolted directly against the existing armour, in others it was spaced in front of the main structure, where it was known as *Vorpanzer*. The order to add extra armour came from Hitler via Field Marshal Keitel on 7 July 1941, when he stated 'The Führer considers it desirable that all new production tanks be radically up-armoured by fitting spaced armour plates … to neutralise thereby the increased penetrating power of the British anti-tank weapons.' It will be realised from this that it was the combat in North Africa, rather than Russia, that was the driver behind the order.

Extra sections of spare track were often employed as additional armour; the fitting of spare links to the hull front was authorised in November 1941 and introduced into production two months later, but the practice pre-dated the order. This may have had some utility when dealing with the less powerful guns of 37–40mm calibre, but increasingly became

redundant when higher-velocity guns firing enhanced ammunition came into use; they did of course retain their usefulness as a means of repairing damaged track. Although not employed much – if at all – in the 1940 campaigns, they were widely used in both North Africa and in Russia. Bars were welded across the front hull nose plate and up to 15 links could be fitted. Some tanks used substantial S-shaped hooks to hang tracks from the steering brake air intake cowls (which of course restricted the airflow to the brakes), and others used thick wire to secure them in front of the vertical hull appliqué. Other shorter sections of track were often secured to the other front

BELOW The later style of driver's visor, which had a 230mm × 50mm opening covered by an armoured glass prism. This gave him a good field of view of about 63°. Above the visor are the two small holes for the driver's binocular periscope, only used when the visor was completely closed. Surrounding it all is a *Vorpanzer* plate.

ABOVE Track links as armour, which added little protection but did improve traction in soft sand. Note that the rubber tyres for the roadwheels have been burned away, revealing the ribbed construction of the steel wheels.
(TM 18/A4)

ABOVE Mounts for the carriage of extra track links were added during production as a standard feature, but this became increasingly less useful as the power of enemy anti-tank weapons increased.

RIGHT Track has been wired to the front of this appliqué – note also the long run of track links on the top and side of the turret.

hull plates, as well as on the turret roof and front sides. Another advantage these would have had that was probably not appreciated at the time was when crossing soft sand: tracked vehicles, unlike wheeled ones, actually benefit from being heavier in soft sand and so traction may have been improved – which must be balanced against the negatives of more stress on automotive components and higher fuel consumption caused by the added weight.

In North Africa, some Panzer IIIs used sandbags as additional protection on the front and sides of the hull, one report used the word 'often' in referring to the practice. Some of them were laid on the roof above the two crewmen in the hull, with care taken not to interrupt the traverse or depression of the gun; the main intention seems to have been to protect the vulnerable area of the turret below the mantlet, but it may also have been done to add to the rather thin armour on the hull roof. The ones on the side were a clear attempt to bolster protection in an area where the plates were known to be thinner. Although not much protection was actually added by this method, the crews at least had a ready source of them to use at night when taking cover in foxholes.

The fitting of additional armour in the form of hull and turret plates known as *Schürzen* (aprons) was first trialled in February 1943, having been proposed as a form of protection earlier the same month. These 5mm-thick unarmoured steel plates (8mm on the turret) were mounted on to frames, with the ones on the hull designed to be easily removed and stowed on the hull for railway movement. The fitting of these was not, initially, to counter shaped-charge (HEAT) warheads; rather, it was to take some of the sting out of normal small-calibre anti-tank weapons, as the sides of the tanks carried much less armour than the frontal aspect (and which is why other tanks with thicker side armour did not need them). The trials were carried out using the Soviet PTRD and PTRS 14.5mm anti-tank rifles as the threat weapons, as well as 75mm HE. Hitler decided immediately that they were to be fitted to all tanks during production, and to retrofit them to AFVs in service. However, when HEAT weapons were then deployed against them, the *Schürzen* were found to be

RIGHT Sandbag protection. This Ausf H *Befehls* has liberal amounts of track added to the turret roof. Protecting a non-traversable turret like this was easier than doing the same on a gun tank, but would be a giveaway to a knowledgeable enemy.

an effective form of defence, as the stand-off between them and the hull rendered the weapons much less effective, often defeating them completely.

Once it was realised by the British in North Africa that the 2-pounder was no longer capable of defeating the Panzer III, except at very short ranges or from the sides and rear, 25-pounder gun/howitzers were pressed into the anti-tank role – a situation that the Germans were familiar with from their First World War experience when 77mm guns were their most effective form of tank defence. The 20lb steel shot fired from 25-pounders using supercharge to obtain the highest possible strike velocity and flattest trajectory, achieved a muzzle energy around seven times that of the 2-pounder. Unsurprisingly the effect of this on the Panzer III (indeed any tank) could be devastating. British trials against a captured Ausf J revealed that 'The structural strength of the hull and turret is quite inadequate to withstand attack from 25-pounder' – even using the normal HE shell could knock a tank out. The Americans found that they could use their 105mm field artillery to the same effect in Tunisia in 1943, although delivered indirectly rather than in the direct-fire anti-tank role.

LEFT The Soviet PTRD anti-tank rifle was capable of penetrating the thin side armour of German tanks and led to the development of *Schürzen*.

BELOW *Schürzen* fitted to the turret and hull of this Ausf L, with the hull mounting rails clearly visible.

BELOW This might be technically termed 'a massive overmatch', but whatever the terminology it would be catastrophic for the crew.

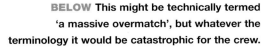

Chapter Four

Weaponry and firepower

Originally intended to be armed with a 50mm gun, the tank went into service with below-par 37mm main armament. Subsequent up-gunning programmes twice extended the life of the tank, as did ammunition improvements, but by 1942 the end of the road was in sight for the Panzer III.

OPPOSITE Although the Panzer III was regularly modified during its service life, the basic features remained remarkably constant, and a crewman would have little difficulty in switching from one model to another. This photograph shows the interior layout of a 50mm-armed Ausf G tank viewed from the loader's side, with the gun travel lock bar in position. *(Tank Museum)*

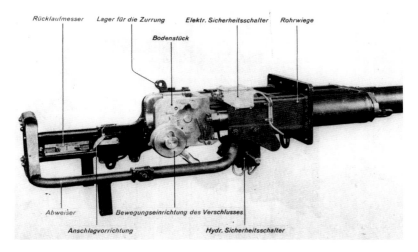

Rücklaufmesser Lager für die Zurrung Elektr. Sicherheitsschalter Rohrwiege
Bodenstück
Abweiser Bewegungseinrichtung des Verschlusses
Anschlagvorrichtung Hydr. Sicherheitsschalter

ABOVE AND BELOW The 'door-knocker' – the 37mm KwK 36. This was fitted from Ausf A to Ausf F, after which it was replaced by the more potent 50mm gun. Note the hinged safety guard behind the gun with the canvas bag for collecting fired cartridge cases.

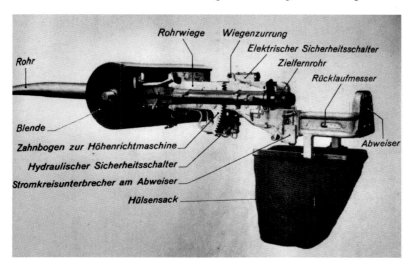

Rohrwiege Wiegenzurrung
Elektrischer Sicherheitsschalter
Zielfernrohr
Rohr Rücklaufmesser
Blende Abweiser
Zahnbogen zur Höhenrichtmaschine
Hydraulischer Sicherheitsschalter
Stromkreisunterbrecher am Abweiser
Hülsensack

120
111
137
116
140
118
117 119

3.7cm KwK 36 main armament

Despite the strongly expressed desire of the officers responsible for developing the new tank to fit a long-barrelled 50mm weapon *ab initio*, it was decided to equip the first models of the Panzer III with the KwK 36, an L/45 weapon with a 1.67m barrel. This was based upon the new and promising PaK 36 gun as used by the infantry. When fitted to the tank using an internal mantlet, the gun could be elevated to +20° and depressed to -10°, which meant that when it came to be used in defensive positions, it could adopt a good fire position that exposed little of the tank to the enemy. When the tank went into action in Poland it had little problem dealing with the enemy armoured vehicles that it encountered, but in France in 1940 it was immediately apparent that it struggled against the better-armoured tanks that it fought there. This was partly due to the small calibre, but also to the rather unsophisticated ammunition used (see later in this chapter). As the weapon itself was not capable of being substantially improved, better ammunition was provided which increased its penetration by about 30%, but it was obvious that it was the gun that needed to be replaced. Luckily the turret dimensions had been designed around the 50mm gun and thus a larger weapon could be fitted with little trouble. By the end of its life the 37mm weapon was being referred to by the crews as a door-knocker – sufficient to alert the enemy to your presence, but not enough to destroy them. It was time to introduce a new gun – in fact, using the same calibre initially proposed. The last two 37mm-equipped tanks were produced in November 1940, with the first 17 of the 50mm models having come off the line as early as July 1940.

LEFT The breech block of the 37mm, stripped down for cleaning. The striker (equivalent of the firing pin) and spring are 116 and 118 respectively. The gun could be disassembled without any tools.

RIGHT The PaK 38, a 50mm anti-tank gun that was adapted to become the L/60 tank gun for the Panzer III. This gun crew is pictured in Tunisia in 1943. *(Bundesarchiv)*

5cm KwK 38 main armament

The design of the 5cm PaK 38 anti-tank had begun in September 1937 but it was not a priority and it was not ready in time to see active service in the French campaign of May 1940, although the first issues seem to have been made just before it ended on 22 June. As a result of the lessons learned there regarding the inadequacies of the 37mm against even medium, let alone heavy tanks, it began to replace the PaK 36 in mid-1940. In June 1940 it was decided to fit a similar weapon to the Panzer III. The same basic breech mechanism was used, but rotated through 90° so that the breech block operated vertically rather than horizontally. It was also converted to use electrically fired cases, rather than percussion, as used on the anti-tank version.

Two barrel lengths of the tank version (KwK) of the 50mm gun were to be produced; the first to be used was the KwK 38, the so-called *kurz* (short) with a length of 2.1m (L/42). This was later followed by the KwK 39 *lang* (long) which used a 3.0m barrel (L/60). Clearly the performance from the longer barrel would be better than that from the shorter one, but initially the longer barrels were solely allocated for infantry-manned anti-tank guns, much to Guderian's fury. There was more to the story than inter-service squabbles, though. One of the design specifications for the L/42 was that for reasons of manoeuvrability its barrel must

CENTRE The breech end of the 50mm L/42 gun, with the canvas bag for spent cases underneath, and the gunner's TZF 5d telescope to the left.

RIGHT The layout of the L/60 breech, with the recoil guard in yellow and the torsion bar system adopted with the longer gun in order to balance the extra weight shown in blue. A recoil indicator is fitted on the inside of the guard (red).

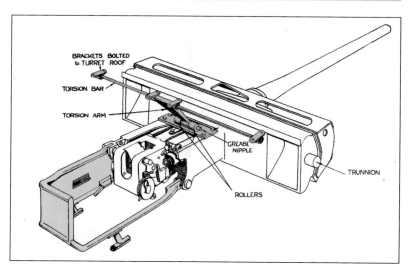

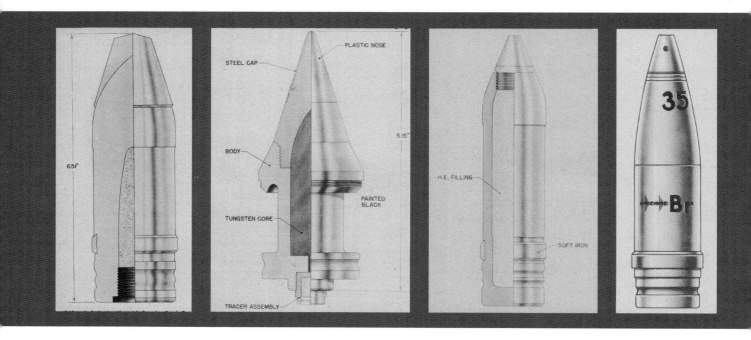

PLASTIC NOSE

STEEL CAP

5.15"

BODY

PAINTED
BLACK

TUNGSTEN CORE

H.E. FILLING

SOFT IRON

TRACER ASSEMBLY

6.51"

35

Br

ABOVE 50mm
projectiles: from left to
right are the *PzGr* 39,
AP40, *SprGr* 38, and
SprGr 41.

not protrude beyond the front hull; although this
may sound strange, at the time it was accepted
design practice to do this, and it was only when
it was realised that the advantages outweighed
the disadvantages that longer barrels were
introduced. Similarly, a short cartridge case was
specified (shorter than the one used on the PaK
38) because of concerns over limited space
within the turret. These two decisions led to a
significantly less powerful design than its towed
anti-tank relative and also negated the desire to
use fully interchangeable ammunition. In terms
of penetrative capability, it was meant to be able
to defeat 40mm of armour at 700m angled at
30° – this was directly related to both the known
protection on French tanks and to the expected
standard combat range that engagements were
thought to take place at.

Sensibly, both the anti-tank and tank guns
used the same family of projectiles, making
production and logistic arrangements simpler,
although the cartridge cases were different, the
L/42 tank gun using a shorter case with much
less propellant.[1] Introducing the 50mm L/42 from
late 1940 gave the Panzer III a new lease of life,
as it finally had a main gun that could do what
the tank had been built for – knocking out enemy
tanks. However, the benefit was not to last very
long. When the first T34 tanks were encountered

in the USSR in July 1941, along with the larger
KV tanks, once again the Panzer III had fallen
behind in the perpetual gun/armour race. There
was only one solution available, as a high-
velocity gun larger than a 50mm could not be
fitted into the tank due to space constraints,
so a way of improving the performance of the
existing weapon had to be found. The barrel
length was finally, and belatedly, increased to
the same L/60 (3.0m) used on the PaK 38 anti-
tank gun, along with increasing the chamber
size to the same 1,250cc as that on the PaK
38. These two changes improved the AP
performance by around 30%.

Because of the increase in muzzle velocity,
the recoil system was modified to cope with
the increased trunnion pull on firing. (A muzzle
brake was considered but rejected on the
grounds of the negative effects on observation.)
But all of this was just delaying the inevitable;
the days of the Panzer III as the German battle
tank were numbered once the T34 appeared.
The design could not be stretched any further
and enemy tanks were mounting increasingly
heavy armour: the British Churchill, introduced
in 1942, sported 102mm of frontal armour that
could only be penetrated at very short range.

The breech mechanism was much the same
on both types of 50mm gun, and indeed the
37mm was little different. Pushing a round into
the chamber tripped the extractors causing the

---

1   Ammunition supply was one of Hitler's constant headaches: German
industry could never meet the demand placed upon it.

LEFT Possibly a trial version of the L/60 gun fitted with a muzzle brake; the service tank used a plain barrel as it was felt that the increased obscuration hindered observation by the crews.
(Tank Museum)

breech block to close behind it. The breech was semi-automatic, meaning that a cam on the recoil guard caused the breech block to open automatically during run-out (*ie* with the gun travelling forward following full recoil), ejecting the spent cartridge case which hit a leather pad on the rear of the safety guard that then fell into a canvas bag suspended underneath. To close the breech on an empty chamber, a lever on the right side of the breech block was operated. The entire mechanism, including the components of the breech block, could be disassembled by hand with no tools needed.

One of the problems that the designers faced when up-gunning their tanks was that Rheinmetall-produced guns tended to have a long length of recoil, making fitting them inside the confines of a tank turret something of a challenge. For example, the 50mm L/42 gun had a recoil length of 335mm, or 13¼in.[2] This recoil length figure is absolutely critical when fitting guns into tanks, and is related to the often-quoted (but much-less-often-explained) turret ring diameter. In simple terms, imagine the gun firing at the horizontal (0° elevation). The rear of the turret can be designed to accommodate both a long length of recoil and the ejection of the spent cartridge case

easily. When the recoil length becomes critical is when the gun is elevated or depressed for firing. It now becomes much harder to ensure that the rear of the gun does not strike the turret roof (firing in depression) or components within the hull (firing in elevation). And this must happen not only when the turret is pointing forward, but throughout the full 360° of traverse. Additionally, the spent shell case must not strike anything that may become damaged when it is ejected – including the crew – and so a guard must be fitted behind the breech, making the internal size of the gun even longer. This was

BELOW The breech ring and block of the 50mm KwK tank gun. Note the 'fqv' manufacturer's code letters, telling us that it was made by Rheinmetall-Borsig.
(TM 1047/A3)

2   For comparison, the post-war British 76mm L23 gun was only 10½in, and the massive 120mm L11 gun only 14in, owing to the fact that they had extremely efficient recoil systems fitted.

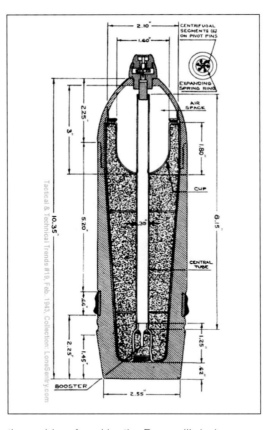

Tactical & Technical Trends #19, Feb. 1943, Collection: LoneSentry.com

the problem faced by the Panzer III designers, exacerbated by the position of the commander directly behind the gun, and the one which sealed its fate. The next anti-tank gun size up, the 75mm, could not be mounted in the space envelope available, whereas in the Panzer IV, which had a slightly larger turret ring, it could. It was therefore decided to rearm the final variant of the Panzer III with the less powerful 75mm low-velocity support gun originally fitted to the

early models of Panzer IV, and rearm the IV with a much longer and more effective 75mm tank gun with a muzzle brake. This represented a complete reversal of the roles of the two tanks, and was a key factor in the decision to stop production of the Panzer III in 1943.[3] Had the tank been equipped with the L/60 50mm gun from the start, as was the original intention, the effects of the T34 when they were first encountered would almost certainly not have been so impressive, as the Panzer IIIs would have been able to destroy them at longer ranges. As it was, the 37mm and short 50mm weapons were no match for the T34, and German tank design was set off on a different path as a result. Thus the final version, the Ausf N, used the 75mm L/24 fire support gun originally seen on early models of the Panzer IV. This weapon was less powerful with a shorter recoil length than its longer-barrelled cousins, and thus could be fitted into the turret of the Panzer III – but only just, as the normal length of recoil was 423mm (16½in), with a ceasefire marking at 455mm (18in). Aside from changing the mantlet to accept the new gun and sighting telescope, and altering the ammunition stowage to suit (64 rounds could be carried) the tank was very similar to the Ausf J, L or M from which it was converted.

7.92mm MG34 light machine gun

The 7.92mm MG34 was developed from the highly effective light machine gun produced for the infantry and the tank version was known as either the *Panzerlauf* or *Panzermantel*. Fitted with a heavy barrel shroud to protect it and with no butt, it fired the same ammunition as the infantry version weapon; early attempts to use double drum magazines within the tank were disliked by the crews, and so the use of 150 non-disintegrating link belts in canvas bags known as *Gurtsack* was standardised.[4] Although the standard ball ammunition designated sS was used, two versions of *Spitzgeschoss mit*

3 A British report of October 1942 commented that 'the tank has by now reached the limit to which it can be developed as regards armour and armament.'
4 The twin drum magazines were developed originally for the Luftwaffe where they were a sensible design in an aircraft being flung around the sky; in a tank they were an unnecessary complication.

Kern (*SmK*), which was AP intended for use against hardened targets, was preferred. Ball ammunition had a green annulus (percussion cap in the base) and a plain bullet. *SmK* with no tracer had a red annulus and a plain bullet, whereas the *SmK* with tracer (*SmK L'spur*) had a red annulus and the forward 10mm of the bullet-tip was painted black. A British report stated that the most common load seemed to be alternately one *SmK* to one *SmK L'spur*.

On tanks armed with the 37mm gun, twin MG34s, slightly staggered, were mounted in their own mantlet to the right of the main gun. The staggered mounting was to allow the drum magazines to be fitted. If required, the guns could be elevated/depressed separately from the 37mm, and fired by the loader opening his lookout in the mantlet; alternatively they could be locked in the coaxial position for the gunner to use. On 50mm-armed tanks only one gun was fitted, leaving a single belt-fed MG34 fixed in the main mantlet. The coax MG was fired using a foot pedal with operating rods, whereas the hull MG was fired directly using the trigger. The ball mount in the hull had an elevation

ABOVE The Panzerlauf version of the MG34, shown with the removable butt fitted. The barrel shroud was of a different design to the infantry version, with its distinctive cooling holes.

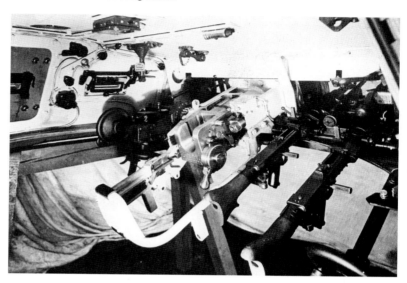

ABOVE The twin MG34 mounting in an early (37mm-armed) turret, which has been placed on a wooden frame, presumably for demonstration purposes. Note the large loader's traverse handwheel, which was simplified on later models. *(TM 2653/C6)*

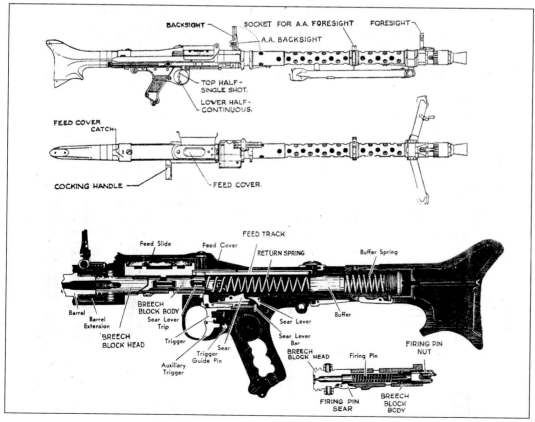

LEFT This is a British illustration of the mechanism of the MG34 (infantry model); note the method of firing single-shot or automatic, by using a different part of the double trigger.

RIGHT The coax MG34 above, and the hull MG with removable butt and bipod below.

BELOW MG34 ammunition boxes. These contained 250 rounds which were broken down into 100- and 150-round belts and stowed in canvas bags along both walls inside the fighting compartment.

Plate No. 17. Coaxial and Hull Machine-guns.

BELOW An early type of square hull MG mounting, later superseded by the *Kugelblende* ball mounting; these were made by the Albach company in Frankfurt am Main.

BELOW A ball-mounted MG34 surrounded by 30mm appliqué armour; making additional armour plates fit around existing components was always a challenge. A British report thought that this *Kugelblende* design was 'excellent', giving faultless protection from bullet splash and being very difficult to jam.

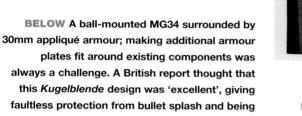

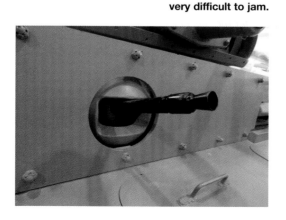

RIGHT An Ausf L: this is the rear of the radio operator's seat seen from behind. Some of the canvas *Gurtsack* for the MG34 can be seen in their stowage racks. A box for MG tools and spares is fitted to the seat backrest. Note the strap securing the loader's traverse handwheel.

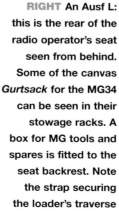

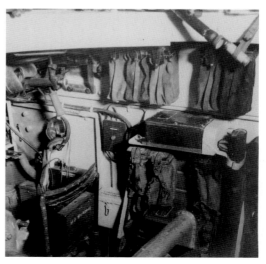

range of +15° to -10°, and a lateral movement of 20° left and right of centre. Both guns used a left-hand feed, and the MG mountings were designed to allow the crews to dismount the guns quickly which, using a kit provided, could then be used outside the tank as a normal LMG, with a clip-on bipod incorporating the front sight, and a butt which slid on from one side and was locked by a spring-loaded catch.

Smoke screening

Smoke screening systems were provided from 1940, intended to allow the commander to build up a local smoke screen that he could withdraw into. For this reason the first type was fitted to the rear right of the hull. Holding five smoke 'candles', each was mounted into a bracket and could be individually released from inside the tank, the same handle being used for all five. Each time that the handle was operated, a ratchet caused one grenade to be ejected away under spring pressure; it was attached to the tank by a thin chain and the weight of it falling initiated a friction igniter in the grenade, allowing the composition to generate a smoke screen. The exposed location was found to be prone to damage and the system was later relocated under the hull rear overhang. The grenades themselves were in the form of a metal cylinder, painted olive green with four interrupted white lines painted around the circumference of the body, like so:

At the top were two circular openings closed off with soldered discs, which were perforated when the grenade functioned and allowed the smoke to issue forth. On later models this system was removed, and a triple-barrelled discharger system was fitted either side of the turret front corners, with the splayed 90mm barrels angled upwards at about 45°. These were electrically fired and propelled K.39 smoke grenades through the air forward of the tank, providing a wide screen between the tank and the enemy without having to reverse into it.

ABOVE No 525, the late Ausf F tank examined in detail for the British technical report in August 1942.

Turret and fire control

A British report of August 1942 described the Ausf F (50mm L/42) fighting compartment as:

Spacious,[5] with the 5cm gun mounted well forward and relatively high in the turret, protected by an external mantlet plate. The muzzle heaviness of the gun is compensated by a lead counterweight fitted to the deflector guard, which is detachable. Another [captured] Pzkw III has a spring-loaded plunger fixed inside the turret to the mantlet behind the trunnions so as to counter the muzzle heaviness. The comparatively thin armour plate protection is on a 30mm basis. On earlier models this necessitated provision of extensive additional protection of an improvised nature; later models carry armour on a 50mm basis, and a special Pzkw III has a double mantlet on the spaced armour principle. There is an absence of power traverse. The mounting of the gun well forward as described appears to make traverse stiff and heavy, but this does not apply to later models.

5   It certainly was spacious with the 37mm gun fitted, but became increasingly cramped as the larger gun breeches were fitted. It would also help to be a small crewman: the author can only just squeeze his 6ft 2in frame into each of the five crew positions.

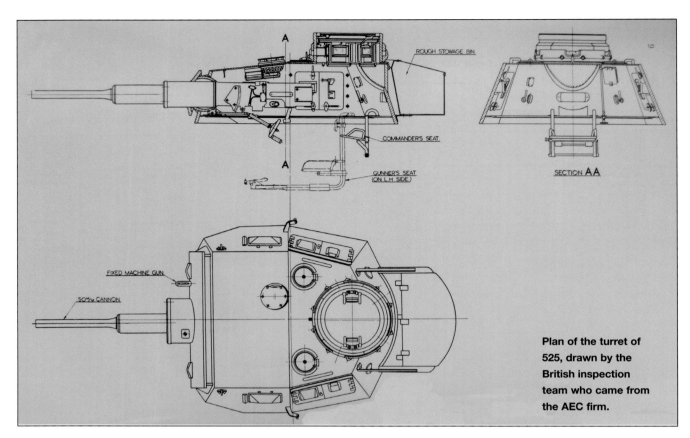

FIXED MACHINE GUN

50% CANNON

ROUGH STOWAGE BIN

COMMANDER'S SEAT

GUNNER'S SEAT (ON L.H SIDE)

SECTION AA

Plan of the turret of 525, drawn by the British inspection team who came from the AEC firm.

RIGHT AND FAR RIGHT The pistol port on the rear of the turret; they were identical on both sides. The lever on the inside rotated against a spring, which moved the port outwards and then swung it to one side. The blue area on the plan shows the actual size of the aperture, designed for an MP38/40 to be sighted and fired through it.

RIGHT The turret side hatches were locked open against these stops, which were fitted with a spring-loaded release plunger.

FAR RIGHT The pistol port open in one of the side hatches.

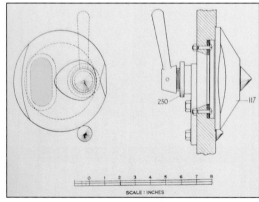

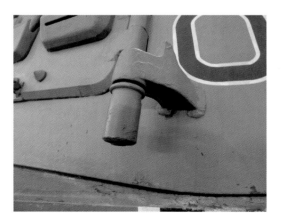

A diagram attached to the report showed the turret ring diameter as 59¾in. It was German policy that 'turret rings were kept as small as possible, and the size was fixed [only] after a space for the crew had been fixed'. The Germans certainly preferred roomy turrets for their crews to work in, hoping that the increased efficiency would outweigh the disadvantages – although once at war, Dr Olbrich of *Wa Prüf* 6 complained that there was a lot of wasted space, that recoil components could be made smaller and that if this was done a much lower turret could be built. However, British tank crews admired the design, having examined German tanks and compared them with their own cramped turrets.

Inside the turret the commander and gunner both sat on seats which were suspended from the turret, as there was no turret basket or rotating floor; the commander sat or stood immediately behind the breech of the main gun, with the gunner on the left alongside the breech. The commander placed his feet on two footrests, one either side of the rotary base junction (RBJ) in the turret floor centre, which revolved with the turret. An extension to the gunner's seat gave him a footrest incorporating the coax MG firing pedal. In some tanks the loader was provided with a folding seat in the right of the fighting compartment, in others it was deleted. In the 12mm-thick turret roof were two circular hinged flaps originally intended for signalling using flags, and in later tanks an electrically driven extractor fan was mounted slightly right of centre above the main gun and coax breeches, with a flat cover on the roof. Large double crew access doors were fitted on either side which could be locked open using a spring bolt, with vision ports immediately forward of them for use by the gunner and loader. A large port in the mantlet to the left of the gun could be placed in one of three positions, and was protected using a 90mm-thick armoured glass prism block (*Schutzglaser* or *Glasblock*) which had a noticeable pale green tint; these were made by Roehm & Haas in Darmstadt. Circular conical pistol ports were fitted either side of the turret rear.

The cast commander's cupola was armoured to a thickness of 35mm, and was closed by two 9mm-thick hatches with rubber padding

ABOVE AND LEFT
Different cupolas shown with the vision apertures both closed and open, which revealed the thick glass prism behind. The pointer in front of the cupola was used to align the gunner on to a distant target. Note also the open signal flag port in the turret roof.

inside; it was fixed to the roof and could not be rotated. Around the cupola sides were five observation ports, each 132mm wide; when open these were protected by armoured prisms and allowed all-round vision – but they required the commander to shift his head around. When they did not need to be locked open, 30mm armoured shutters acting as a visor closed over them, being operated together by a handle inside. Each prism was surrounded by a rubber eye and nose guard (or brow pad). Marked above the prisms was a ring known as

ABOVE The forward-facing vision block in the cupola, with the central sighting lines, used in conjunction with the external pointer. Either side of the glass blocks are rubber pads and the levers for operating the armoured shutters can be seen under the blocks.

BELOW The mechanism of the 12-hour clock indicator, showing the rotating driveshaft connected to the turret rack which positioned the ring (red) inside the cupola.

BELOW RIGHT The gunner's turret direction indicator disc.

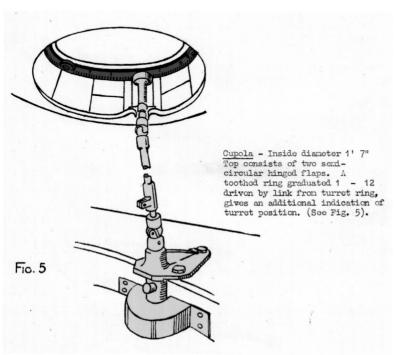

Cupola – Inside diameter 1' 7"
Top consists of two semi-
circular hinged flaps. A
toothed ring graduated 1 – 12
driven by link from turret ring,
gives an additional indication of
turret position. (See Fig. 5).

FIG. 5

the 12-hour clock indicator. This showed the orientation of the turret relative to the hull (gun front being 12 o'clock) and the gunner had a smaller version of the dial to his left, making it easier for the commander to give fire control orders and directions to the gunner, for example 'traverse right to 2 o'clock'. A vertical pointer on the turret roof just forward of the front port allowed the commander to line the gun on to a distant target from inside the cupola, using two vertical lines marked on the inside of the forward-facing vision block.

Sighting

The gunner sighted using a ×2.5 telescope fitted to the left side of the gun mounting. This was very well protected as externally the object lens was inside an 18mm hole in the mantlet; for additional protection a piece of 10mm steel was fitted inside the mounting just in case a bullet or fragment managed to enter the aperture. A number of different models of telescope were used and the Leitz-made TZF5 seems to have been the most common: the 5a model was used with the 37mm, the 5d with the L/42 and the 5e with the L/60. The gunner rotated a dial to set the range and weapon ordered by the commander, it being indicated by a vertical pointer in the 12 o'clock position.

He then aimed at the target using the centre of seven triangles in the graticule pattern; the three smaller triangles either side were 4 mils[6] apart and were there to allow for the effects of crosswind and for aiming-off at moving targets.

The hull machine gunner used the ×1.8 *Kugelzielfernrohr* KZF2 cranked telescope made by Zeiss for sighting his gun, which looked through a 10mm hole drilled through the gun mounting. The articulation of the telescope was deliberate, as although it complicated manufacture it allowed the gunner to adjust the eyepiece to suit his height: another example of the German insistence on crew comfort and efficiency. Control of the gun was by moving a headpiece which he wore all the time, so that the movement of his head also moved the gun, leaving him hands-free a lot of the time – useful as his main role was of course as the tank's radio operator. Firing the gun used the normal double-crescent trigger, although usually it would be used in the fully automatic mode.

Turret traverse

Traversing the turret was by means of a two-speed traverse handwheel in the gunner's position. He would select either *langsam* (slow) or *schnell* (fast) by operating a push/pull lever on top of the traverse gearbox, and then traverse the turret using his right hand in response to the commander's orders. A trigger mechanism on the handwheel fired the main gun. A linkage went across the turret from the gearbox to the loader's side, where another traverse handle (*hilfsantrieb*) was provided. Sometimes described as the emergency traverse handwheel, it seems likely from the name that the original intention was to allow the loader to assist the gunner when a large angle of traverse had to be covered quickly: the turret was out of balance with all the weight in the front half, and as no power traverse was ever provided, traversing it quickly often required a lot of muscle. Also in the loader's position was a lever operating a plunger to lock the turret into the gun front position. To elevate or depress the gun, the gunner used his left hand on an elevating handwheel; on non-tactical moves the gun could be secured in one of two positions

6   17.8 mils = 1 degree.

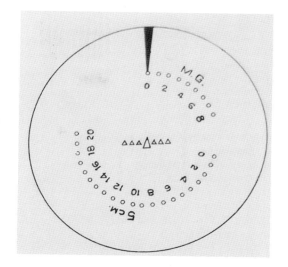

LEFT The 50mm graticule pattern; the 37mm version was of similar design but had a maximum range of 1,200m.

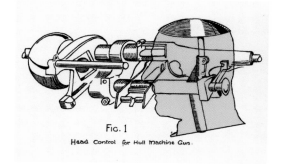

Fig. 1

Head Control for Hull Machine Gun.

ABOVE, LEFT AND BELOW The hull MG mounting was a complicated design, using a balance spring to take the weight of the gun and mounting, so that the radio operator could move it using his head.

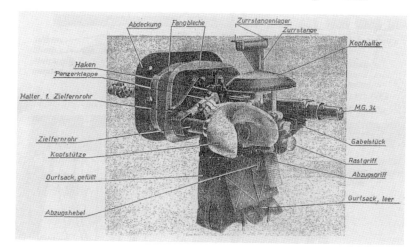

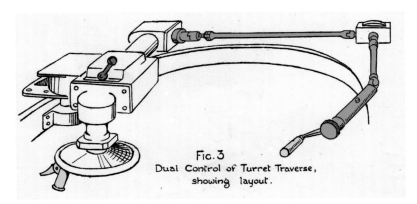

Fig. 3
Dual Control of Turret Traverse,
showing layout.

ABOVE The *hilfsantrieb* traverse handle showing the linkage to the traverse gearbox; later tanks did not have this fitted, although it is not clear if this was a factory or a field modification. The lever shown in purple is the fast/slow traverse selector.

(horizontal or elevated) for travelling, using an internal strut secured to the turret roof.

Firing the main armament

Firing the main gun used an electrical circuit, with an emergency back-up provided; this was selected by the gunner using a switch on the turret wall marked *Netz* (normal circuit) and *Not* (emergency). The normal circuit took power from the batteries via the turret lighting circuit and when the gunner pressed the firing switch, the circuit would be completed only if both of

the two safety switches (one electrical, one hydraulic) were made, delivering the current to the electrical primer on the base of the cartridge case. The hydraulic safety switch was linked to the oil-filled recoil buffer and stopped the gun firing if buffer oil was too low, because excessive recoil would be dangerous to the commander who of course was positioned immediately behind the gun. The electrical safety switch was fitted to the right side of the cradle for use by the loader. This was 'made' by pressing a red button, and the indication F (for *Feuer* or Fire) appeared in a window. Each time the gun recoiled, the switch was broken showing the indication S (*Sicher* or Safe), requiring it to be made each time. If for any reason the main vehicle batteries failed, selecting *Not* would use a small emergency 'pocket' battery within the selector box, which had sufficient power for a few more shots.[7]

Protecting the gun from the deleterious effects of sand was important in dry, dusty conditions. A cardboard muzzle cover was developed, which was reinforced with a waxed fabric; it fitted tightly over the muzzle of the gun and was designed so that in action it could be fired through without having to remove it. Additional weapons carried in North Africa were reported as being a P08 (Luger) for each crewman, plus two MP40 sub-machine guns and a 27mm signal pistol.

Ammunition

German tank guns started the war able to fire only two main types of ammunition: AP (*Panzergranate* or *PzGr*) and HE (*Sprenggranate* or *SprGr*). The *Panzergranate* design of ammunition was the German designation for Armour Piercing Capped (APC). This was an AP shot with a pointed ballistic windshield over it to give it better performance; it was also filled with an explosive bursting charge, designed

---

7   A very similar system to this was adopted on the British 120mm gun used on Chieftain.

— Elektr. Sicherheits-schalter

— Bodenstück

— Bewegungseinrichtung des Verschlusses

— Hydr. Sicherheits-schalter

— Verschlußkeil

— Abweiser, abgeklappt

LEFT The open breech of the 37mm KwK, with S showing (for *Sicher* – Safe) on the electrical safety switch box (*Elektr. Sicherheits-schalter*). The recoil guard has been 'broken' at the hinges to allow more room in the turret when not in action.

to improve the effects inside the target after penetration had been achieved. Early German policy was to use APC ammunition with a small bursting charge, as it was believed that plain AP shot could penetrate straight through without causing any real damage. The 50mm version of this ammunition was tried out against two Crusader tanks in a British trial in Egypt in January 1942; the conclusion was that, 'The German 50mm APC projectile is more likely to initiate fires [within the target] than either the 2-pounder or the [US] 37mm shot, because of the bursting charge which distributes the hot fragments over the interior of the tank.'

Armour-piercing

Improved AP performance came in the form of the *Panzergranate* 39 design; this was the German designation for armour-piercing capped ballistic cap (APCBC) and which gave a moderate increase in penetration. Another real advance came with the *Panzergranate* 40 design. This was the German designation for Armour Piercing Composite Rigid (APCR), which used a tungsten carbide (TC) sub-calibre core to improve performance; this was surrounded by a lightweight metal or plastic body to bring it up to full calibre, and it had a pointed ballistic cap for the maximum aerodynamic efficiency. In German it was also called *Hartkernmunition*, literally hard-core ammunition. The lighter projectile could be fired at a higher velocity than the normal AP ammunition, increasing performance and thus extending the service life of the gun firing it. The 37mm *PzGr* 40 was introduced just prior to the French campaign, and although it gave increased penetration at short ranges, it was forbidden to be used beyond 300m as it was no better than the *PzGr* 39 above that range (owing to the velocity rapidly declining beyond that range, with the equivalent loss of penetration). With the 50mm gun, the adoption of the *PzGr* 40 ammunition in the L/42 version meant that its 20mm-diameter TC core could penetrate 53mm of armour at 750 yards, whereas if using the *PzGr* 39 the range at which 53mm could be reliably defeated was reduced to 250 yards. The downside was that both the accuracy and penetration of the 50mm *PzGr* 40 fell off rapidly after about 600m, whereas *PzGr* 39 could be used out to around 1,000m, as it lost velocity less quickly.

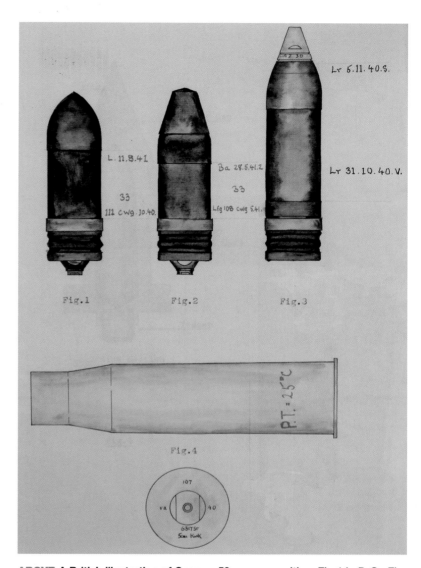

ABOVE A British illustration of German 50mm ammunition; Fig 1 is *PzGr*, Fig 2 is *PzGr* 39, both using a yellow tracer. Fig 3 is *Sprenggranate* – HE. Notes attached to the original sketch state that the HE projectile was painted dark green, but which turned black after exposure to the sun.

BELOW The arrowhead shape of the *Panzergranate* 40 ammunition family made it very distinctive. Although good at short ranges, its velocity and therefore penetration fell off rapidly.

TABLE 5A: AMMUNITION PROJECTILES

Calibre/Gun	Type	Projectile weight complete (lb)	Explosive content (oz)	MV (fps)	MV (mps)
37mm L/45	*SprGr* 18 (HE)	1.37	1.0	2,690	820
	SprGr (HE)	1.4	0.87	2,690	820
	PzGr (APC)	1.5	0.42	2,625	800
	PzGr 40 (AP40)	0.79	0	3,450	1,052
50mm L/42	*SprGr* 36 (HE)	3.94	5.87	1,476	450
	PzGr (APC)	4.56	0.87	2,240	683
	PzGr 40 (AP40)	1.87	0	3,444	1,050
50mm L/60	*SprGr* 36 (HE)	3.94	5.87	1,804	550
	PzGr (APC)	4.56	0.87	2,700	823
	PzGr 40 (AP40)	1.87	0	3,930	1,198
75mm L/24	*SprGr* 34 (HE)	12.6	1.44	1,378	420
	GrPatr HL (H/C)	9.75	NK	1,476	450
	NebelGr (Smoke)	13.7	0	NK	NK
	PzGr 39 (APCBC)	15.0	NK	NK	NK

High-explosive

The other type of ammunition used was high-explosive or HE. Two types of 37mm HE shell were used, each weighing 1.4lb in total. In both, the HE content was tiny, carrying either 28g (early) or 24g (later) of PETN or TNT explosive; an aluminium band was painted on the olive-green projectile to allow it to be easily recognised in poor light. The larger 50mm HE projectile weighed about 4lb, of which less than 10% was explosive, and left the gun at 450mps (L/42), or 550mps from the L/60. Equipping

BELOW The 37mm *SprGr* HE shell contained a small amount of explosive. Two slightly different versions were used, as seen here.

BELOW The British sketches of the *PzGr* 40 projectile, often referred to as arrowhead for the obvious reasons ... its performance fell off rapidly above 600m.

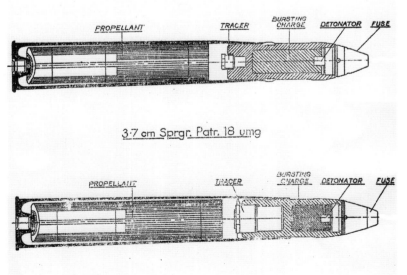

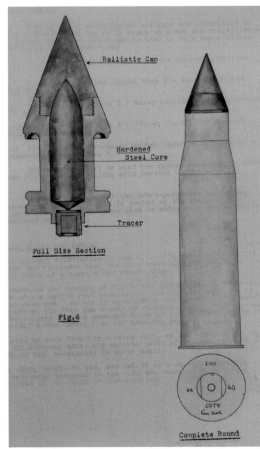

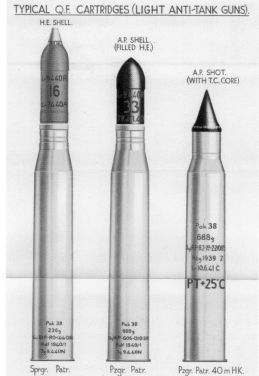

TYPICAL Q.F. CARTRIDGES (LIGHT ANTI-TANK GUNS).

H.E. SHELL.

A.P. SHELL.
(FILLED H.E.)

A.P. SHOT.
(WITH T.C. CORE)

Sprgr. Patr.

Pzgr. Patr.

Pzgr. Patr. 40 m HK.

the tank with an HE round, small as it was, was a wise decision, as it allowed the tanks to engage small targets like A/T guns against which a kinetic energy AP shot would have little effect, and it also meant that they could fire at a greater range; in theory this was 6,500m but in reality out to around 2,500m.

As mentioned earlier, for reasons of standardisation, the same projectiles were used on both types of 50mm guns, with the L/42 using a shorter cartridge case with less propellant. The L/60 50mm used exactly the same ammunition as fired by the PaK 38 anti-tank gun, save that the tank version used an electrical primer in the cartridge base, whereas the PaK used a traditional percussion primer; these could be easily swapped in the field. Despite the same projectiles being used, improved AP performance was obtained from

the L/60 in comparison with the L/42 because of two related design features. Firstly, it came from the longer barrel which gave an increase in projectile velocity – the standard shot went from 683 to 823mps through the longer barrel, an increase of nearly a third. Secondly, it also came from a larger chamber capacity which

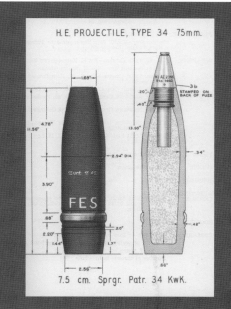

H.E. PROJECTILE, TYPE 34 75mm.

7.5 cm. Sprgr. Patr. 34 KwK.

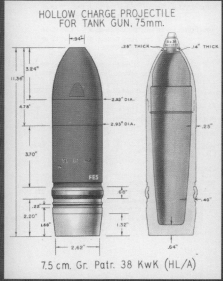

HOLLOW CHARGE PROJECTILE FOR TANK GUN, 75mm.

7.5 cm. Gr. Patr. 38 KwK (HL/A)

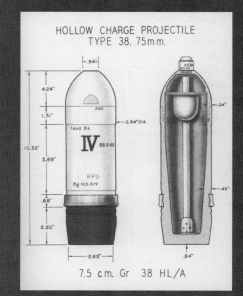

HOLLOW CHARGE PROJECTILE TYPE 38, 75mm.

7.5 cm. Gr 38 HL/A

allowed more propellant to be fitted into the cartridge case, from 794cc to 1,250cc, about 57% larger. When the L/60 gun was introduced, ammunition stowage was reduced from 99 rounds to 84, still a healthy amount.[8] (For comparison, the US Sherman M4A1 carried 90 rounds and the British Cromwell V only 64.) Ammunition loads would vary depending on the type of operation being undertaken, but a 60/40 spilt between HE and AP seems common, and within the AP load more *PzGr* 39 were generally carried than *PzGr* 40.

Hollow charge

When the 75mm L/24 gun was mounted on the Ausf N it came, not surprisingly, with a family of ammunition that had been developed over the years for that weapon mounted in other vehicles. While the prime function was to deliver an HE shell, it had been realised that this left any vehicle equipped with it vulnerable to attack by an enemy tank. As the L/24 barrel was too short to allow the development of an effective AP projectile – the muzzle velocity being too low – an alternative route was taken. This led to the development of the *Hohlgranate* (hollow shell), or shaped-charge projectile. The hollow charge (H/C) principle utilises the Munroe effect, in which a cone-shaped explosive charge is initiated at a stand-off distance from the target. Unlike the kinetic energy ammunition used with AP, its effectiveness does not diminish with increased range as it is not dependent on strike velocity for its effect, although the Germans limited its range to 1,500m owing to the problems of hitting a small target above that range. When the ammunition was first developed there was anxiety over its use, lest the Russians should discover its secret and develop their own version – one of the perpetual problems with new weaponry. Codenamed *RotKopf* (Redhead) probably owing to the copper liner inside the nose, Hitler placed an embargo on the use of the ammunition which was not lifted until about Christmas 1941. When the Ausf N conversion programme started in June 1942, the 75mm hollow charge ammunition was already in service and so those tanks would have carried a proportion of their

ammunition load of 64 shells as *Hohlgranaten*. A smoke shell was also carried.

Ammunition performance

This area is somewhat contentious, as different sources give quite a wide variety of claimed penetrative performance for Second World War weapons. Table 3B is thus an attempt to summarise the likely average performance of the weapon/ ammunition combinations used. These figures are approximations and should be treated with a degree of caution, as a number of factors meant that crews could not rely upon them to guarantee a penetration in combat. A rule of thumb used during the war allowed comparisons to be made between the standard angle that armour was set at and used in trials (30° to the vertical), and other angles, to account for differences in the way that armour was sloped on real tanks. If the strike on a plate was absolutely perpendicular to the surface (0°), then penetration increased by about 1.25. If the armour was angled at 60°, the expected penetration would be reduced by half. As an example, if a 100mm plate set at 30° could just be penetrated, then at the same range the same ammunition could be expected to penetrate 125mm at 0°, but only 50mm at 60°. Although only an approximation, this of course shows the effectiveness of sloping armour, something that the Panzer III did not utilise.

Possibly more relevant are the results of some firing trials conducted by the Germans in North Africa against a captured Matilda II, which sported a maximum armour thickness of 78mm on the front of the hull nose and 75mm on the turret and driver's vertical plate. Using both the 50mm KwK L/42 and the L/60, the results were translated into ranges at which the crews equipped with those weapons could expect a successful penetration. With the L/42 the hull front could be defeated from 250m, and the turret side from 350m. With the L/60 the equivalent ranges were 500m and 600m respectively. Unfortunately the exact ammunition used was not stated, but interestingly, the additional range generated by the longer barrel appears

---

8   For some reason, British reports considered that fewer were carried than this: 75 and 66 respectively for the L/42 and L/60.

TABLE 5B: TANK GUN PERFORMANCE

Calibre	Weapon	Barrel length (calibres)	Ammunition	MV (fps)	Range (m)	Penetration (sloped 30°) mm v rolled homogeneous armour
37mm	KwK 36	L/45	PzGr	2,625	100 500 1,000 1,500	34 29 22 19
			PzGr 40	3,450	100 500 1,000	64 45 34
50mm	KwK 38	L/42	PzGr 39	2,240	100 250 500 750 1,000 1,500	56 53 48 44 36 28
			PzGr 40	3,444	100 200 300 400 500 750 1,000 1,500	95 83 73 64 58 53 42 26
	KwK 39	L/60	PzGr 39	2,700	100 500 1,000 1,500	67 57 44 34
			PzGr 40	3,930	100 500 1,000 1,500	130 78 44 32
75mm	KwK 37	L/24	Hohlgranate	1,476	N/A	British estimates were that the hollow charge shell would penetrate 45mm if the armour was struck at 30°, and 55mm if struck perpendicularly.

Sources: *Illustrated Record of German Army Equipment Vol II* (Pt 1) and *Vol III*. John Salt, 'Second World War anti-tank weapons penetration', available at: http://mr-home.staff.shef.ac.uk/hobbies/ww2pen3.pdf.

much more pronounced than if one looks at the official performance figures; the implication here was the L/60 was around 50% better than its older, shorter cousin. The tests also concluded that the Matilda turret front was immune, possibly because of the additional protection provided by the mantlet in addition to the turret armour behind. Separately to this, a British trial conducted for broadly the same reasons believed that the L/42 could penetrate the front of a Grant (with 57mm on turret, and 63mm equivalent on hull front) at up to 600 yards, whereas the L/60 increased that range to almost 1,000 yards, again indicating an actual performance increase of around 50%, although different ammunition used could have been a factor. The key point here is not whether these figures were totally accurate, but that they were used by crews in action as a guide to decide when to open fire. (In 1940 instructions had been issued that Panzer III crews were not to open fire with the 37mm at ranges above 600m, not because of issues with penetration, but because it was seen as a waste of ammunition owing to inaccurate range estimation.)

Chapter Five

Panzer III walkaround

The Ausf L owned by the Tank Museum is in excellent (near-original) condition following a restoration project, which is a tribute to the work and dedication of the museum's professional and volunteer staff. Photographed by Matt Sampson, this walk-around chapter gives readers a superb insight into a typical Panzer III operated in North Africa in mid-1942.

OPPOSITE **The Tank Museum Panzer III after restoration.** *(Tank Museum TM 10138/071)*

ABOVE Right side profile. *(TM 10138/104)*

RIGHT Left side profile. *(TM 10138/101)*

ABOVE Looking inside the engine compartment right-hand side: the fuel filler neck (without the rubber sealer) sits on top of the fuel tank, with the Maybach TRM engine in the centre. The oil-bath air filters are mounted above, with the trunking which brings the air from the fighting compartment. *(TM 10138/164)*

ABOVE RIGHT A close-up of the Maybach manufacturer's symbol and engine instruction plates. *(TM 10138/165)*

RIGHT Looking from the turret into the engine compartment, with the two access plates opened; the cut-outs in the hatches allowing air to circulate can be seen, as can the batteries in the left-hand side. Unlike the Ausf F described in Chapter 3, in this Ausf L both batteries are mounted together alongside the engine. *(TM 10138/170)*

RIGHT The rear hull was used for the cooling components, and on the left-hand side we can see one of the cooling fans and drive belts. *(TM 10138/172)*

ABOVE The shaft for connecting the starting handle to the Bosch inertial starter is shown here, with the exhaust pipes running downwards towards the exhaust silencer boxes in the centre. *(TM 10138/173)*

ABOVE Looking at the rear hull overhang from underneath: the exhaust silencer boxes are either side of the towing bracket, and the five containers and chains for the smoke candles are between the grills. On earlier tanks these were mounted on the rear hull right, but were prone to damage. *(TM 10138/174)*

BELOW Looking into the turret from outside the cupola. A wealth of detail can be seen, including: the gun alignment 'sight' on the forward-facing periscope; the gunner's bucket seat; the commander's footrests in the centre; and the rear backrests for the driver and radio operator. The handles underneath the periscopes control the opening and closing of the armoured visors.

ABOVE Looking at the cupola from outside, the five glass prisms with the rubber bump pads between can be seen. These were not periscopes, but were direct-view devices protected by armoured visors. The very small space between the rear of the 50mm gun recoil guard and the commander's position can be appreciated.

BELOW Looking up at the underside of the cupola from the loader's position. The commander's seat and rudimentary backrest are at bottom centre, with the 12 o'clock indicator mechanism also visible.

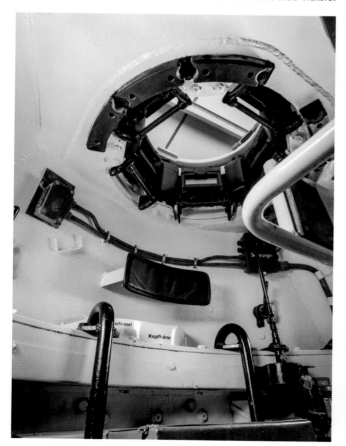

ABOVE The breech of the 50mm gun taken from inside the gun guard. Visible on the roof is the torsion bar system used to balance the gun, and the ventilation fan fitted to remove fumes from the turret guns.

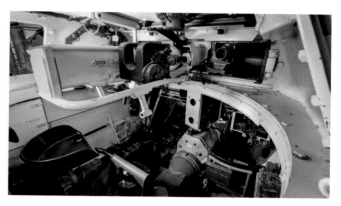

ABOVE The loader's side. The breech and recoil guard for the 50mm gun dominates the turret, and the lack of a rotating floor means that there is a lot of space – although the reader must remember that three men with their kit would soon fill this up!

BELOW The breech ring has been repainted in an incorrect colour; it seems likely that originally it would have been left in bare metal. The coaxial MG is not fitted, but the mounting for it can be seen to the right.

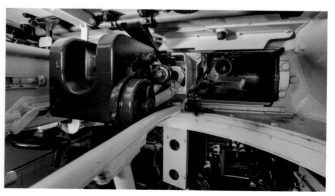

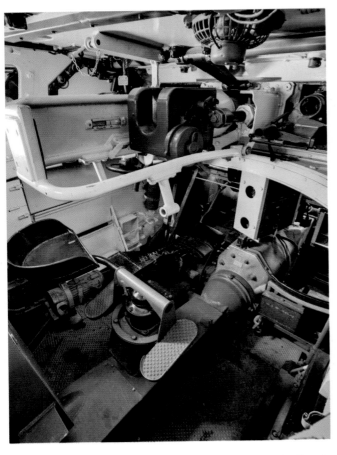

ABOVE Mounted above the transmission tunnel on the floor is the rotary base junction, the means whereby electrical power was transferred between the hull and turret. This rotated as the turret was traversed, which turned the commander's footrests with it. To the left side is the gunner's bucket seat and footplate.

BELOW Looking forward into the gunner's position. He is protected from the gun's recoil by the guard to the right, which reminds the crew that the air pressure in the recoil recuperator should be 32kg/cm². To his front is the sighting telescope eyepiece and browpad, with the traverse and elevation handwheels beneath.

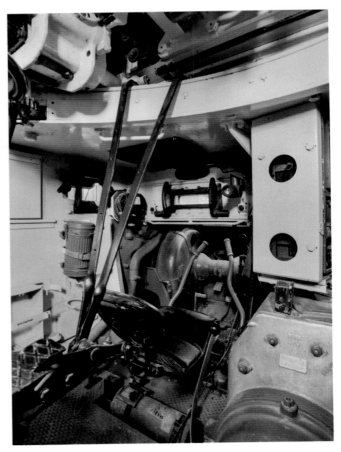

ABOVE Extending from the turret sill are two beams to support the front of the gunner's footplate, which included the foot pedal for firing the coax MG. Forward is the driver's position, with his personal gas mask case strapped to the hull wall alongside.

BELOW Ducking underneath the 50mm gun reveals the driver's (left) and radio operator's (right) positions. Dominating the centre is the rear of the ZF six-speed gearbox, with the FuG 5 radio mounted above. The configuration shown here is not typical: the transmitter is mounted above the receiver, whereas it should be fitted in front of the radio operator under the hull roof.

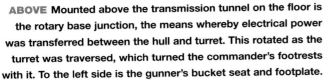

ABOVE The driver's position. His steering tillers are either side of the seat, with the gear-change lever to his right. The instrument panel (without speedometer) is mounted above the gearbox and his glass block prism for driving is immediately in front. When the armoured visor was closed, the binocular eyepieces were swung across to the left to allow him to drive while protected.

RIGHT On the right front of the hull is the radio operator's position, complete with hull-mounted MG34 in its complicated head-controlled mounting. Note the vision port and prism to his right.

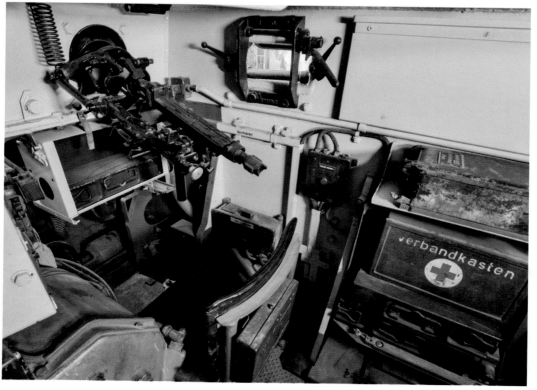

LEFT The backrest of the radio operator's seat was lifted in and out of the frame to allow him to take his place – and of course get out quickly in an emergency. The box on the hull side wall next to the backrest is the radio control box that his headsets and throat microphone would connect to.

LEFT Don't listen to anyone who tells you that the front hull hatches were for the crew – they allowed access to the final drives and front of the gearbox. The driver's tillers can be seen, but there is obviously insufficient space for even the smallest crewman to get in or out of.

BELOW Looking into the turret from the left-hand side – this side hatch was used by the driver and gunner ...

RIGHT ... and from the right; this hatch was used by the radio operator and the loader.

BELOW Inside the turret with the side hatches closed – the insides were painted the same colour as the main external colour for camouflage reasons.

BELOW LEFT Mounted on the right side of the rear bulkhead is the mechanism for releasing each of the five smoke candles in turn.

BELOW On the inside of the gun safety guard is the recoil indicator, showing the length of recoil in centimetres. Marked at 33.5cm is FEUERPAUSE (ceasefire), informing the crew to stop firing as recoil was dangerously excessive. The same distance was used on the shorter L/42 gun, telling us that the recoil system on the more powerful L/60 had been made more efficient in order to keep the recoil length the same and allow the larger gun to be fitted into the turret.

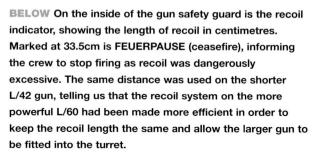

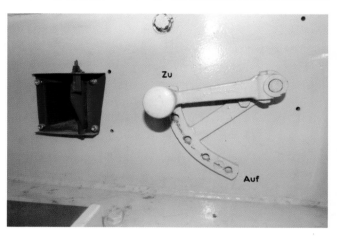

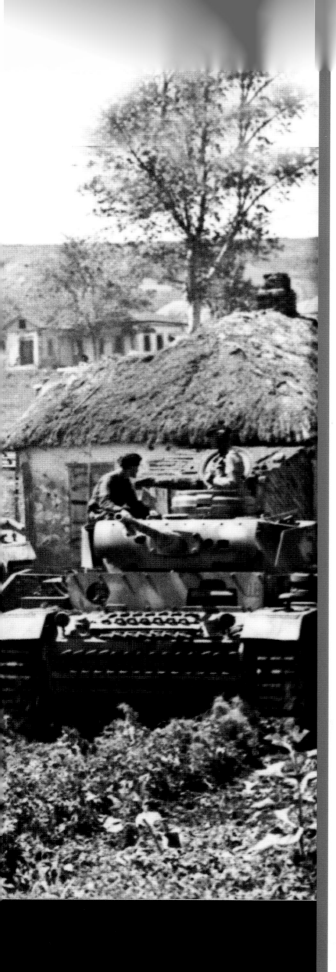

Chapter Six

The Panzer III in action

In combat almost continuously from 1939 until at least 1944, the Panzer III formed the backbone of the panzer divisions in its role as the main gun tank. Combat experience in 1941 in the USSR and North Africa indicated that it was being outclassed by more modern designs and the Panzer III's use declined thereafter.

OPPOSITE Midsummer 1943 and four brand-new looking Panzer III Ausf L or M advance in Russia. These tanks are carrying the full suite of hull and turret *Schürzen* armour. By this time the days of the Panzer III as a gun tank were all but over, although the chassis would continue to be used as the basis for a large number of variants and conversions. *(Bundesarchiv Bild 101I-219-0595-20)*

Introduction

Because of the nature of the war fought by Germany, it is a reasonable assumption that almost all of the Panzer IIIs built were used in action, and the vast majority were destroyed as a result, with only a handful existing in museums – although occasionally examples are recovered after years of being underwater or buried in mud or ice. In this chapter we shall investigate the campaigns in which the Panzer III took part, with a clear focus on the use of the tank in those theatres of war:

for those who wish to know more about the campaigns in detail, this is not the place to look. Initially, each of the two *Panzer Abteilungen* (battalions) in a Panzer regiment would have four companies – in addition to the battalion HQ and the *Stabs* (staff) company. The Panzer III was the main equipment in three of the companies, which were known as light companies, whereas the fourth company was the support company operating Panzer IVs with the short L/24 75mm weapon; this led to the initial production ratio of building three Panzer IIIs for every Panzer IV. Therefore the Panzer III companies would be numbered 1 to 3 (1st *Abteilung*) and 5 to 7 (2nd *Abteilung*). The rationale behind mixing the tanks in this way was that the Panzer IV would exist solely to support the battle-winning Panzer IIIs by providing them with on-call HE, as well as being able to engage targets beyond the range of the Panzer IIIs' 37mm; it was absolutely not an infantry support tank as used in the French and British armies.

Turret numbers were used to identify the company (and therefore battalion), platoon and then individual vehicle number. Regimental commanders generally used R01, and other tanks within the regimental headquarters used R02, R03, etc. Battalion command tanks used a Roman numeral I or II followed by 01, 02, etc. Company commanders would use the company number followed by either 00 or 01, so the company commander of the third company would use either 300 or 301. Tank platoons usually consisted of five tanks, therefore the third digit would range from 0 or 1 (commander) to 4 or 5 (junior NCO), although there were numerous (pun intended) variations to this, dependent on the unit, the campaign, the date

RIGHT The turret being removed from a 37mm-armed tank, which has seen some heavy action. Because the turret was not fitted with a rotating cage and turntable, this was a fairly simple task. *(Tank Museum)*

etc. The most common painting style was a red or black inner with a white outline, but other colours were used inside, as were white outlines with the inner in the vehicle colour, plain block letters in a range of thicknesses and plain green was often used when the vehicle was painted in a sand colour scheme. And of course some vehicles were not marked at all.

Poland and France, 1939–40

By the time Germany invaded Poland (*Fall Weiss* or Operation White), six panzer divisions were in existence. The vast majority of the 2,500 or so tanks deployed by the Wehrmacht in Poland were Panzer Is and IIs, augmented with Czech-made 35(t) and 38(t).[1] On 1 September 1939, the first day of the invasion, only 87 Panzer IIIs were in front-line service, the majority within the 1st and 3rd Panzer Divisions, with 11 held elsewhere. Some 26 of these tanks were reported as being destroyed in the course of the Polish campaign, with another 60 or so requiring major repair afterwards – in total, just about 100% of the tanks involved.[2] The combat losses were caused mainly by anti-tank weapons that were able to penetrate the tanks' thin armour, and the repair bill speaks volumes for the state of reliability of the Panzer III at that time. After the Polish campaign ended, Germany's tank forces were in a poor state. In total the army only held 2,701 serviceable tanks, the vast majority of which were Panzer Is and IIs. By the first day of the new year, the overall number of Panzer IIIs in service was only one more than had started the campaign in Poland (see Table 6A).

---

1   1,445 Panzer Is and 1,223 Panzer IIs (total 2,668) were in service, but not all were committed to the operation. In addition 196 of the 35(t) and 78 of the 38(t) were used in Poland.

2   One report stated that in total, the German army lost 674 tanks during the campaign, though many of these were repairable; 45 Panzer IIIs and IVs were noted as having been totally destroyed. A rule of thumb figure that is sometimes useful is that for every tank totally destroyed, two others would be disabled but repairable.

BELOW Another tank in need of repair: the idler has been removed from 12, and the tank has been 'half-tracked' to allow it to be moved under its own power. *(Tank Museum)*

TABLE 6A: DISPOSITION OF PANZER IIIS, 1 JANUARY 1940

PANZER DIVISION	PANZER III HELD
1	38
2	13
3	12
4	12
5	13
TOTAL	88

BELOW An Ausf E crossing an obstacle – note the logs carried on the rear decks, common practice to allow the tanks to cross marshy or boggy ground. *(TM 1048/D2)*

It is worth noting that as early as September 1939 the army clearly realised that its thin armour made the Panzer III vulnerable, and recognised that the armour would often be penetrated. For these circumstances, repair instructions were issued stating that penetrations of less than 20mm could be filled with weld, whereas larger holes should be bored out in order to accept a pre-made armoured plug in various thicknesses and diameters of up to 100mm, which could be inserted into the hole and then welded into place. If cracking along a joint had occurred, it was to be strengthened if possible by welding a piece of armour plate on the inside.

Between February and April 1940, it was ordered that those Ausf A–D that had taken part in and survived the campaign were to be withdrawn from front-line users and returned to ordnance, being replaced by newly produced Ausf Es and Fs. (This was not the end of the road for the development tanks though, and a few D models were shipped out to North Africa the following year with the 15th Panzer Division.)

Before the 10 May 1940 attack on the Low Countries and France, Hitler had told his generals that 'The tank arm must be used for

RIGHT The Panzer III was anything but invulnerable, and its thin side armour was a particular weakness. *(TM 3142/B2)*

ABOVE Recognition crosses used in Poland – it was suspected that the original white versions were used as aiming marks by the Polish gunners, and so were subdued using yellow paint. Later the outline version was used instead.

LEFT They may have been right – two shots have penetrated the thin side of the superstructure, including one which almost certainly would have killed the driver.

operations for which it is best suited. Under no circumstances must the tanks be permitted to become entangled in the endless confusion of rows of houses in Belgian towns.' In this he was undoubtedly correct, not only in terms of using relatively thin-skinned tanks in street fighting in which they would be vulnerable to infantry anti-tank rifles fired at short range, but more generally. Tanks had weaknesses as well as strengths, and it was important not to view them as the panacea for all battlefield tasks. At the start of the campaign against France (*Fall Gelb* or Operation Yellow) 349 Panzer IIIs were available (see Table 6B for their disposition – 39 Panzer III command vehicles were used, but it is not clear if these were included in that total or

not). During the course of the Battle of France, only 65 replacement Panzer IIIs were issued, although after the campaign had finished a report gave the figure of 135 Panzer IIIs written off: 84 in May, the remainder in June.[3] Thus 33% of all the Panzer IIIs used were written off. These figures indicate two potential problems: either new tanks were not being produced fast enough to match losses, or the nature of the campaign meant that replacement tank issues simply could not keep up with the movement of the forces. As no new issues at all were made in June or July either could be true, although

3   Another source stated 109 Panzer IIIs written off but only 71 replacements issued; whatever the true figure, the moral of the story is the same.

LEFT 'Under no circumstances must the tanks be permitted to become entangled in the endless confusion of rows of houses in Belgian towns.' Hitler's directive could not always be followed, as this 12th Panzer Division tank demonstrates. *(TM 3088/C3)*

TABLE 6B: DISPOSITION OF PANZER IIIs, 10 MAY 1940

PANZER DIVISION	PANZER REGIMENT	PANZER III HELD
1st	1st	28
	2nd	30
2nd	3rd	29
	4th	29
3rd	5th	0
	6th	42
4th	35th	20
	36th	20
5th	15th	24
	31st	28
9th	33rd	41
10th	7th	29
	8th	29
	TOTAL	349

the first reason seems to be the key one. At the end of the campaign the overall strength of the *Panzerwaffe* had decreased by 13% – but Hitler clearly realised the advantages that the tanks had brought to the campaign. On 23 June he ordered that 35 infantry divisions were to be disbanded or placed into suspended animation, but that the number of tank and mechanised divisions was to be doubled, which of course meant an increase in production of the Panzer III. However, this was offset to some degree by another change of direction ordered by Hitler on 12 July, giving priority of weapons production to the Luftwaffe and the Kriegsmarine to allow them to attack Britain – something the army could not do without mounting an invasion. This meant the shifting of steel from army contracts which prevented the army from increasing tank production and modernisation – including the programme to replace the Panzer III's 37mm gun – which (unbeknown to most) was to be urgently required in 1941.

A post-operation army report following the French surrender stated:

With their greater manoeuvrability, cross-country mobility and speed, the German PzKpw III and IV are superior to all French tanks except the super heavy. This superiority will be complete by significantly improving the armour and equipping the

PzKpw III with the 5cm tank gun, after which, both of these tanks could be regarded as excellent. The French Somua [S35] is superior to the PzKpw III in both armour and armament (4.7cm gun), but its poor mobility and manoeuvrability negates both these advantages.

Another report noted:

The 37mm KwK in the Panzer III is unsuitable as an armour-penetrating weapon. The head of OKH had requested that introduction of the 50mm KwK in Panzer III production be accelerated ... the earliest start for production of Panzer III with 50mm is crucial.

Luckily for the crews, the installation of the new gun meant that a new external mantlet was also required (it had already been designed by Krupp) and this increased the armour protection on the frontal aspect of the turret to 50mm. The problems of inadequate gun power are well illustrated by this story of a German action during the battle for France:

In the early morning of 17th May, Hauptmann Friedrich Huschenbeth was commanding the 7th Light Company in the 2nd Abteilung of Panzer Regiment 1, part of 1Pz Div. After only one week of combat he appeared to have only six tanks in his company, including his own. His company was in reserve, advancing westwards from Dercy, between St Quentin and Reims. By midday the company was astride the Crecy-sur-Serre road, with three of its Panzer IIIs facing forwards (westward), and the other three covering their rear. Enemy tanks were then reported over the radio, and a heavy Char B1bis tank named 'BOURRASQUE' appeared. This had 60mm of frontal armour and was armed with a 75mm gun in the hull, plus a 47mm anti-tank gun in the turret. The forward three Panzer IIIs opened fire and scored multiple hits, but the French tank continued on its course, despite being subsequently engaged by the rearmost platoon as well. The 37mm rounds were hitting but failed to penetrate the thick armour. After destroying a German armoured car, it was engaged by a 20mm Flak gun and by engineers and infantry using hand grenades, also without effect. Huschenbeth decided to manoeuvre his tanks to attack the beast from the more vulnerable rear, and with two of his Panzer IIIs opened fire at around 200–250m. The Char shrugged off these attacks, despite being hit many times on the turret and hull rear. After knocking out an unarmoured car, the five-man French crew then decided to abandon their tank, as two had been wounded by fragments. It was subsequently discovered that the abandonment was mainly due to the tank being immobilized, as the engine had been damaged by the solitary hit that had penetrated the armour (although a French report later stated that it had run out of fuel). Hauptmann Huschenbeth was killed in action five days after this battle.

From this we can appreciate the frustration that the German tank crews must have felt when hitting the monster but being unable to penetrate it. They must have been thankful that the French tank seems to have been handled poorly and was not turned upon them – unless of course this was attempted and they used their much better mobility to avoid it. We should also note that the new *PzGr 40* ammunition did not start to be issued until June, so we must assume that the earlier 37mm APC ammunition was being used. Whatever the exact circumstances, the lesson to be learned was clear: Germany's primary battle tank was armed with a weapon incapable of destroying the heavy tanks that its enemies were fielding. In a similar vein, an interim report issued by 3rd Panzer Brigade during the battle – on 4 June 1940 – made the point that the only reliable anti-tank weapon was the short 75mm KwK gun firing the *PzGr 39* (APCBC) ammunition. It said that the 37mm was 'ineffective against the Somua at normal combat ranges … the 37mm ammunition did not meet expectations and is considered as inadequate for use against modern enemy tanks'. (The Char B1bis had not been encountered by this brigade, and the 75mm would have proved ineffective against that tank if it had.) As a result of the combat experienced in France, once the campaign was

concluded the following equipment requests were made regarding the Panzer III:

- Mounting a more effective weapon (47mm or 50mm) is urgently needed. In comparison to the other requests, this is viewed as having top priority and the greatest urgency.
- Due to continual stoppages, the MG34 is not usable in combat in its current form using drum magazines.

As we already know, both of these suggestions were to be implemented. The same report also suggested that the installation of a rangefinder in Panzer IV was 'desirable'. It is interesting to note this request as the use of a rangefinder for Panzer III was not mentioned, presumably because the ranges it was firing at were less than those of the Panzer IV. However, this was somewhat short-sighted. As the calibre and performance of tank guns increased, so too did

ABOVE Undergoing extensive repairs, this Panzer III demonstrates how the tank could be stripped apart for overhaul. Getting the necessary spare parts was another thing entirely. *(Tank Museum)*

BELOW An Ausf F with the distinctive open mantlet and twin MG34s used on the 37mm-armed tanks. The crew are driving with one of the front hatches open, probably to aid cooling.

ABOVE The adoption of the L/42 50mm gun made a difference, but it was still not the long gun that Hitler had ordered. Note the roadwheel missing on this Ausf J.

the effective ranges, and equipping the primary battle tank with a rangefinder would have delivered benefits in terms of ammunition saved and more effective engagements.

By the end of June 1940 the only opponents left fighting Germany were the British. As their experience from 10 May onwards had been that of one long retreat, they were unable to capture even a solitary example of a German tank in order to send it to the UK for evaluation, whereas the Wehrmacht had hundreds of

British tanks to examine, including all the latest models. Therefore the Germans knew what they needed to do to improve the Panzer III, by up-armouring it but also and most crucially by fitting the 50mm gun that Guderian and others had wanted from the start. The tank was then ready for its next test, which was to take place in an unexpected area.

North Africa, 1941–43

As early as autumn 1940 the Germans were conducting contingency planning in case they needed to send forces to Libya to support – meaning prop up – their Italian ally. Initially, 3rd Panzer Division was stood by for the task, but the lukewarm reaction from Mussolini led to it being stood down, although elements from the division were later deployed as part of 5th Light Division. On 9 January 1941 Hitler stated that he intended to send armour to 'block' the British. He was not so much interested in the Italians being militarily defeated as he was in the political ramifications of such a defeat, fearing that it would topple Mussolini. Two days later he issued Directive No 22, ordering the preparation of a *Sperrverband* or blocking detachment for movement to Tripoli. On 3 February he directed the Wehrmacht to send the *Sperrverband* to Libya, and without consulting the army high command decided that Rommel was to command the force. *Unternehmen Sonnenblume* (Operation Sunflower) was the codename allocated for the operation. On 19 February the force was given the name *Deutsches Afrika Korps* (DAK), a title that would go down in history, not least because of Rommel's aggressive, often foolhardy, handling of it. He was ordered to block further British advances westward, and to be prepared to assume offensive operations to recapture Cyrenaica in due course. Of course, as we all know, he disregarded his orders and immediately went on the offensive. The British view of what he was likely to do was much more realistic than Berlin's orders; in a 5 March intelligence report issued just after the arrival of the Germans, the three tasks identified for the DAK were:

■ Ensure the safety of Tripolitania (western Libya)
■ Recapture Cyrenaica (eastern Libya)
■ Invade Egypt.

BELOW In May 1941 the British produced this recognition poster of the Panzer III, which noted its vulnerabilities, including the ability of the 2-pounder to penetrate its sides and the joints between the hull, superstructure and turret. *(Tank Museum)*

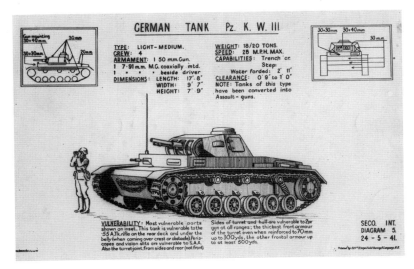

Two Panzer III-equipped regiments were sent to North Africa, and both were in Libya by early May 1941. The first to go were Lieutenant Colonel Olbrich's Panzer Regiment 5, part of the 5th Light Division (which was renamed 21st Panzer Division on 1 October). Having been one of the units warned for deployment to Libya the previous October, the regiment were able to move quickly and arrived in Tripoli on 10/11 March 1941. Apart from its other tank and vehicle types, it was initially equipped with 71 Panzer IIIs. The majority were Ausf Gs, but it also had a few Fs, plus four or five of the newest H models (J production had only just started). On the way, a fire on the merchant ship *Leverkusen* in Naples harbour led to the loss of ten of these, but they had all been replaced with F and G models by 29 April. On 31 March 1941 it was still awaiting two of the replacements, as it had reported the internal distribution of its Panzer IIIs as follows:

- Regimental HQ – 1
- Staff Company – 2
- 1st Abteilung   1st Light Company – 17
- 1st Abteilung   2nd Light Company – 16
- 2nd Abteilung 1st Light Company –16
- 2nd Abteilung 2nd Light Company – 17

The first Panzer III to be lost in the campaign was destroyed after it strayed on to an Italian (!) anti-tank mine on 24 March; it caught fire and was burned out, and examination showed that the damage had split the weld seams on the front hull. The first loss from enemy fire took place a few days later at Marsa el Brega, in an engagement with 5RTR who were attempting to block the German advance in order to allow the 1st Armoured Division to withdraw. Two Panzer IIIs

BELOW One of the DAK Panzer IIIs being loaded at Naples (with Vesuvius in the background) for transportation to join Rommel's armoured forces in North Africa. Note the jerrycan stowage on the turret roof, indicating that this tank has already been prepared for tropical service, although it still appears to be in Panzer Grey paint. *(TM 73/G6)*

ABOVE In order to make it appear that he had a huge fleet of tanks, Rommel may have recalled the Reichswehr experience when he ordered the building of canvas dummies mounted on to *Kübelwagens*. These were rudimentary close-up, but were only intended to fool British air reconnaissance. They were *not* fooled – a report stated that 'Dummies of this type so far seen have not been very convincing.' *(Tank Museum)*

ABOVE AND BELOW Classic views of the Panzer III in action in the North African desert. *(TM 142/A1 and Bundesarchiv)*

ABOVE Variations of the DAK symbol used on many vehicles in North Africa, as well as the smaller, more discreet divisional signs.

(and one Panzer IV) of the 2nd Abteilung of Panzer Regiment 5 were knocked out, their fuel tanks being hit and the tanks burned out. For the loss of the three tanks the British lost five, which may have seemed a favourable rate of attrition at the time, but would increasingly be seen as unsustainable in view of their overwhelming material superiority of the British.

The second Panzer III unit to arrive was Panzer Regiment 8, part of 15th Panzer Division, equipped with 61 tanks of various models: 51 Ausf Hs, 5 older Ds and 5 Es. Almost all had been fitted with the additional 30mm appliqué armour. The unit unloaded in Tripoli between 25 April and 6 May. By this time a total of 132 Panzer IIIs had been shipped into the theatre. The appearance of German tanks with a 50mm gun came as a rude shock to the British, who were dismissive of the capabilities of the 37mm tank gun following their experiences in France, but who were nowhere near getting their own 6-pounder (57mm) gun into service.

In mid-1941 a German report noted the positives and negatives of the tanks that they had deployed. The Panzer IV was noted as having no major problems, whereas the Panzer III attracted the following comments:

At first there were too many breakdowns. Now it is a good vehicle suitable for the tropics. The new, wider tracks have proved to be successful, [with] less roadwheel wear. Due to continuously sucking in dust, the engines are usually completely done-in [by] 1500 to 2000kms, pistons with 2 to 3mm play. The air must be drawn in from the crew compartment through larger oil bath filters. After a 40km desert journey the oil bath filters must be thoroughly cleaned. A modification has been initiated. The main deficiency is insufficient filtering of the engine intake air. High wear on the roadwheels of those with wider tyres and narrow tracks. The same modifications to the suspension as on the Ausf H is already arranged. It is to be accomplished during general rebuilds back in Germany.

The reference to the suspension modifications probably means the new style of sprockets and idlers, although it could also mean the later type of shock absorbers. This should have come as no surprise to the readers of the report: tanks that were sent to the heat and dust of the desert would clearly require some modifications to make them more reliable in those conditions – it should be remembered that the tank had been designed for central European conditions, with no thought given to extreme climates.

ABOVE Monday 5 October 1942: a genuine photograph of a Panzer III exploding. Australian soldiers beat a hasty retreat when they realised that the tank they were investigating was about to explode! *(Australian War Memorial)*

RIGHT Living in the desert was tough, whichever side you were on. One crew member keeps watch while the remainder keep cool under the shade of a canvas awning. The colour of the tank and the surroundings suggest that this photograph was taken in Tunisia rather than Libya, probably in 1942. The nearest crewman is wearing a one-piece overall. *(Topfoto/Ullstein Bild)*

BELOW A well-known but rare colour image of a Panzer III in North Africa. The crews preferred to travel outside the tank when not in action, and large amounts of fuel and spares were consumed in these administrative moves.

ABOVE If only … a captured Panzer III (probably Ausf H or J) is recovered using an American-made Diamond T tank transporter. The Germans lacked the ability to emulate this, which meant that their tanks had to drive large distances, burning precious fuel and leading to increased breakdowns. *(TM 1721/C5)*

As an expedient measure, five holes were cut out of the rear engine hatches to increase air circulation and thus improve cooling; later production tanks had raised 16mm steel air intake louvres mounted on the engine decks to protect the engine – the British christened these 'table tops'. Poor air filtration had a terrible effect on engine life. Whereas a tank engine in normal conditions could be expected to last for up to 3,000km, in the desert it would require replacing after only half that, and spare engines were hard to come by. This was

LEFT AND BELOW Knocked-out Panzer IIIs in the desert. One has a projectile stuck in the muzzle, reportedly caused by an internal explosion setting off the ammunition in the breech. *(TM 2382/E2 and AWM)*

ABOVE The *einheitskanister* or jerrycan; the pressed sides made the container stronger and also allowed for expansion and contraction of the contents. On the left is another type of German 20-litre fuel container. *(Arche-foto)*

critical in keeping the small amount of panzers operational; the more that the German tanks had to travel on their own tracks, the worse the situation became. With Rommel's success in pushing eastward towards Egypt came a penalty, as the tanks were 'burning up' engine life in just moving, rather than conserving it for fighting. Unlike the British, the Germans did not own a fleet of tank transporters, which saved the huge expenditure of track mileage necessary when moving large distances east and west as the battles ebbed and flowed.[4]

From September 1941 the tanks were modified with a curved flap added under the rear hull overhang above the exhaust silencer to deflect the air exiting downwards from the radiators and which was thought to increase the amount of dust being thrown up. Because of the limited range of the Panzer III, it was found to be necessary to fit a rack to the rear of the tank's hull, able to carry ten *einheitskanistern*, better known as the jerrycan. The extra 200 litres thus carried added about two-thirds to the tank's range. Some tanks also carried jerrycans on the turret roof for use during road marches, but these were discarded if possible before going into action. Access to the fuel tank was gained by raising the front right-hand engine hatch; the filler had a large rubber mouth about 8in across to help reduce spillage, and when the engine deck was closed above it the weight bore down on the rubber, sealing the filler.

4   The SdKfz 9 with SdAnh 116 trailer was used for battlefield recovery, but not for moving tanks over long distances.

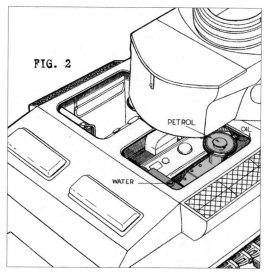

ABOVE Occupying Vichy France following the Operation Torch landings in November 1942, this Panzer III is waiting to be refuelled. Note the circular stain on the inside of the engine deck, caused by it bearing down on the rubber ring around the petrol filler. *(Tank Museum)*

ABOVE AND BELOW Inside the engine compartment, showing the fuel filler and radiator header tank filler. *(TM 1047/A6)*

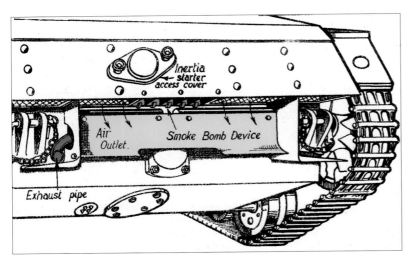

Air
Outlet.
Smoke Bomb Device

Exhaust pipe

ABOVE The curved flap (yellow), used to deflect cooling air exiting the engine compartment so that less dust was kicked up, betraying the tank to the enemy.

BELOW This member of the Royal Gloucestershire Hussars does not seem too impressed by the Mk III Special.
(TM 2357/C4)

The 30mm armour basis on the earlier tanks, before they were up-armoured, could be vulnerable to 2-pounder AP shot at up to 1,500m,[5] if the projectile struck the armour perpendicularly or close to it (known as 'normal' by gun designers). This range would have decreased significantly had the plates been sloped, as sloped armour has the effect of both increasing the apparent thickness and in increasing the chance of a ricochet. However, the basic design of the tank could not be easily amended, and the fitting of appliqué armour in increasing thicknesses went a long way to reducing vulnerability. It was not until the British 6-pounder gun and US 75mm guns were introduced in 1942 that the Germans again

5 2-pounder Mk 2 AP shot could penetrate around 40mm at 1,000yd (at 30').

began to feel that they were under-armoured in North Africa.

Replacement tanks and spare parts were hard to come by, particularly once Operation Barbarossa was in full swing and the Germans were encountering harder fighting than they had anticipated. It was noted that 'hardly any German tanks reached Libya between the end of June and 19 December 1941'. At the very end of 1941, 44 Panzer IIIs (and 16 Panzer IVs) were sent out as replacements; as a German report stated that the first Ausf Js reached North Africa in late 1941, these may have been them. Some 76 Ausf L tanks mounting the L/60 were sent to the DAK between July and August 1942. These tanks, when first encountered by the British at the Battle of Gazala in summer 1942, were referred to as Mk III Specials – the British immediately recognised the significance of the up-gunning programme. Not surprisingly they were sent straight into action, and despite their firepower advantages they were not invulnerable; 175 Panzer III losses were recorded between 26 May and 20 July 1942: 161 L/42, and 14 L/60 – the latter losses clearly occurring rapidly after their first use. On 23 July 1942 21st Panzer Division reported that it only held 22 serviceable tanks – enough for about one strong company. This comprised 12 Panzer III and six Panzer III L/60, plus four other unspecified types. One Panzer III L/60 was in workshops for a short-term repair, and another five Panzer IIIs and four Panzer III L/60s were in for longer repairs.[6]

Between the commencement of the Second Battle of Alamein on 23 October 1942 and 2 December, the DAK had written off (as totally destroyed) another 161 Panzer IIIs: 94 armed with the L/42, and 67 of the precious L/60 'Specials', leaving only 31 Panzer IIIs operational. During Alamein, the strength of the two panzer regiments was reported on two dates, as shown in Table 6C.

The first five days following the British attack had been particularly hard: Panzer Regt 5 lost 18 of its L/42 and 20 L/60 by 29 October, representing 44% of the start state. By 2 November, Pz Regt 5 had lost 51% of its Panzer IIIs, and Pz Regt 8 had lost 52% – hard

6 Short-term usually meant less than two weeks and long-term 15 days or more.

TABLE 6C: OPERATIONAL PANZER IIIs DURING EL ALAMEIN

	23 October 1942			2 November 1942		
	Panzer III L/42	Panzer III L/60	Operational/Held	Panzer III L/42	Panzer III L/60	Operational
Pz Regt 5 (21st Pz Div)	43 (out of 53)	43 (out of 44)	86/97	28	20	48
Pz Regt 8 (15th Pz Div)	38 (out of 43)	43 (out of 44)	81/87	15	27	42

fighting indeed. In the following month, another 59 tanks were written off, meaning that the Panzer III force was down to only 17% of its start strength, comprising only eight L/42 tanks and 22 L/60s (ignoring other types of tank). It is a tribute to the determination, stamina and resilience of the troops that the campaign did not end there and then. The German high command was equally determined that resistance must continue, and following the Operation Torch landings conducted by the British and Americans in early November 1942, reinforced the Tunisia garrison. In November 1942 Panzer Abteilung 190 was sent to Tunisia; in late February 1943 it was renamed the 2nd Abteilung of Panzer Regt 5. Between November and December 1942 Panzer Regt 7 of 10th Panzer Division was also sent to Tunisia; 16 of its Panzer IIIs were lost in transit, the sea crossing from Italy becoming increasingly dangerous as the campaign progressed. In total, in the six months between 1 November 1942 and 1 May 1943 the Wehrmacht shipped 68 Panzer IIIs (probably mostly Ausf L and N) and 142 Panzer IVs to Tunisia, of which 16 and 28

respectively were lost in transit, representing 21% losses en route. Another more important point emerges from these statistics: although the availability of tanks might have come into it, the proportional increase in the supply of Panzer IVs represents the shift that was happening across the Wehrmacht: the Panzer III was no longer regarded as the primary battle tank.

Between late November 1942 and 24 January 1943 *Schwere Panzer Abteilung* (heavy tank battalion) 501 was transported to Tunisia.[7] In addition to its 20 Tigers, 16 Panzer III Ausf Ns were sent. These were used to support the Tigers in much in the same way that the Panzer IV had been designed to support the Panzer IIIs, and apparently they were successful in that role. A report noted that the Ausf N 'has proved to be very successful in engaging mass targets with *Sprenggranate* [HE]. The effectiveness of the *Hohlgranate* [hollow charge projectile] has not been established.' This last comment was simply due to the fact that the Panzer IIIs had not

---

7   It later changed designation to become the 3rd Abteilung in Panzer Regt 7.

LEFT Ausf N No 832 knocked out in Tunisia, which has the turret-mounted smoke dischargers but the two-piece commander's hatch, a typical mixture of features that serve to confuse the identification issue. The spare track links appear to have been painted in the camouflage colour.

(yet) been required to engage Allied tanks, the Tigers being designed for the job. A single Tiger company of *Schwere Pz Abt 504* was then sent to Tunisia in March, and we can assume that it would have taken its normal complement of ten Panzer III Ausf Ns with it. British reports often referred to the Ausf N as Mk III CS, using the British abbreviation for close support. Also in Tunisia, a completely burned-out Panzer III Ausf M was discovered by British troops in April 1943, who noticed the special arrangements that the M had for deep wading and thought this worthy of a report, proving that at least some examples of the final model of the gun tank were sent to North Africa.

One source records that 839 Panzer IIIs (excluding command tanks) were sent to North Africa over a period of around two years, with the models varying from a handful of Ausf Ds to the Ausf Ns with the Tiger battalions, and everything in between. The majority of these were replacement tanks, rather than ones shipped as part of a unit move. At least 78 were lost in transit, meaning that if these figures are correct 761 actually fought during the campaign. In comparison, just over 300 Panzer IVs were shipped, making the Panzer III the most important tank used in the campaign. Indeed, over the course of its service history, the North African campaign was the only one in which the Panzer III was the dominant German battle tank from start to finish.

In all the studies commissioned by the British to report on captured Panzer IIIs in North Africa, all noted the absence of radios. It is unlikely that they were taken as souvenirs, as more attractive items remained in the tanks, and therefore we can conclude that either the Germans were particularly good at removing radio sets when tanks were abandoned (often under fire), or that more likely there was a serious shortage of radios in the DAK. It is often illuminating to consider what the people on the other end of a tank battle thought about their opponents and the tanks they used. We have already considered quite a few official reports, but let us now look at an unofficial view. The 9th Queen's Royal Lancers were part of the British 2nd Armoured Brigade for most of the desert campaign. Their regimental history records the following:

We received an unexpected visitor – Mrs Clare Booth [sic] of the American Press. The Adjutant had to answer some very-much to the point questions, not the least awkward being: 'How do you account for the recent defeat of three famous cavalry regiments?' The only possible answer was to ask Mrs Booth to examine first an American Honey and then a German Mk III which we had found and towed into leaguer. She took a ride in the Honey, looked at the Mk III, and said 'Yes, I see.'

A penetration test was carried out against the German Mk III. The 2-pounder on the Crusader and the 37mm on the Honey did not make more than a shallow impression on the front plate at four hundred yards. Even at one hundred yards they failed to penetrate the lower plate, but did so on the upper one. The results were depressing, and the Brigadier was invited to have a look. It must be remembered that at this time we were hopelessly behind the Germans in armour, firepower and reliability. The 2-pounder tank gun was a miserable little thing, its shells simply bounced off the standard Mk III, and the German panzer crews treated it with contempt. Their high-velocity 50mm gun cut easily through Crusader and Honey alike. They could sit down comfortably at fifteen hundred yards and with their magnificent telescopic sights pick off British tanks at leisure.

At the very end of the campaign, the final tank strength report issued stated that in Tunisia 44 Panzer IIIs (plus 25 Panzer IVs and one Tiger) were still operational.

Yugoslavia and Greece, 1941

In order to crush Yugoslavia and Greece, two German armies were deployed. The German 12th Army was one of the two allocated to the task, with four panzer divisions included in the order of battle: 2nd, 5th, 9th and 16th. This formation was the one which invaded southern Yugoslavia on 6 April 1941, and having dealt with that country, wheeled south to mete out the same punishment to

RIGHT A *Panzerbefehlswagen* III in Yugoslavia. Note the track links carried on the front and the large box on the rear decks; Panzer IIIs had little stowage for the crew and they frequently took to stowing additional items on the engine decks. *(Bundesarchiv)*

CENTRE This enterprising crew have constructed a wooden box within a metal frame to stow at least some of their kit. The YI symbol indicates 8th Panzer Division. *(Tank Museum)*

BOTTOM A 2nd Pz Div gun tank in Greece in April 1941. It is not a camouflage pattern on the front, but merely mud and dirt running off the track links. Note the Allied soldier prisoner on the rear deck. *(Bundesarchiv)*

Greece, which capitulated on 23 April. Invading Yugoslavia from the north was the 2nd Army, which included three panzer divisions: 8th, 11th and 14th. Although only 21 Panzer IIIs were written off during the campaign (out of 56 tanks of all types that were lost), the effects of the long distances and mountainous terrain affected the rest of the fleet, with all of the tanks requiring up to three weeks of workshop overhauls afterwards to get them ready for future operations. The braking systems were particularly affected by the gradients that had to be negotiated. Although impossible to quantify, this repair bill must have had a negative impact on the German invasion of Russia in June, if for no other reason than the amount of spare parts used up for the maintenance and repair of seven divisions' worth of tanks. Indeed, it was this more than any other single campaign that made the Germans realise that their spare part provision was inadequate, and by then it was too late to rectify.

Barbarossa and the Eastern Front

When Hitler decided to attack the USSR, the Panzer III quite naturally was the tank used to spearhead the advance. Although it had already been decided to rearm all of the earlier 37mm models with the 50mm gun in June 1940 – a year before the invasion – large

TABLE 6D: PANZER DIVISION STRENGTHS, JUNE AND SEPTEMBER 1941

PANZER DIVISION	22 JUNE 1941			10 SEPTEMBER 1941		
	TOTAL HELD	37mm	50mm	OPERATIONAL	LOST	NOT OPERATIONAL BUT REPAIRABLE
1st	71	0	71	43	15	13
3rd	110	29	81	6	35	69
4th	31	31	0	24	22	59
9th	71	11	60	31	14	28
10th	105	0	105	75	19	11
11th	71	24	47	21	24	33
13th	71	27	44	37	10	26
14th	71	15	56	49	17	9
16th	71	23	48	26	36	9
17th	106	0	50	20	39	37
18th	114	99	15	30	21	83
TOTALS	892	259	577	362	252	377

numbers still remained unconverted. Expecting a short campaign, and completely unaware of the heavily armoured tanks possessed by the Red Army, the decision was made to delay the conversion until 'the campaign in the east is concluded. Preparations for the offensive make it necessary to interrupt this programme.' This optimism condemned the crews of 259 Panzer IIIs to start the new war with the door-knocker as their main gun, ineffective against their opponent's newer tanks and unable to deliver a decent-sized HE shell. Their losses in comparison to the better-armed tanks can only be guessed at, but their vulnerability probably meant that few survived long enough to be converted as planned.

Looking at the casualties within a tank regiment of two battalions over a short period can be instructive. Here we will look at Panzer Regiment 4 in Pz Div 13, and its tank casualties over a four-day period, very early in the Russian campaign. The regiment started the attack with an impressive 158 tanks: 9 Panzer Is, 45 Panzer IIs, 27 Panzer IIIs with 37mm, 44 Panzer IIIs with 50mm L/42s, 20 Panzer IVs, and

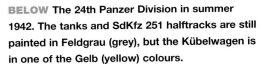

BELOW Possibly *the* classic image of the early Russian campaign: German infantry using the tank for cover during the advance of summer 1941. The tank commander is sensibly keeping his head down. *(Topfoto/ Ullstein Bild)*

BELOW The 24th Panzer Division in summer 1942. The tanks and SdKfz 251 halftracks are still painted in Feldgrau (grey), but the Kübelwagen is in one of the Gelb (yellow) colours.

13 command tanks. From this start state of 71 Panzer IIIs, the regiment reported the figures of Panzer IIIs still operational as follows:

24 June 1941 am – 34
24 June 1941 pm – 12
25 June 1941 am – 12
25 June 1941 pm – 5
26 June 1941 am – 5
26 June 1941 pm – 7

What is really interesting is how quickly the unit was depleted by both battle casualties and breakdowns, and how ineffective the ordnance organisation was in replacing unserviceable tanks. These figures for the morning and evening also indicate that not only were the units not fighting at night, but also that it was difficult for the Germans to increase their strength, either by repairing tanks or getting replacements, during the hours of darkness. On a larger scale, in the 272 days between the first day of the invasion, 22 June, and 20 March 1942, the Germans had lost a total of 3,319 panzers (ie those of German manufacture) of all marks. In return they had received only 732 replacements, a shortfall of 2,587. Although this was offset to some degree by the fact that many of the tanks lost were Panzer Is and IIs, and which were replaced by the more capable IIIs and IVs, it was clearly an intolerable

ABOVE The expectations of a quick victory over the USSR had been destroyed by the winter of 1941, but it was in the terrible fighting in Stalingrad a year later that it became clear to many that victory in the war was beyond Hitler's reach. This bullet-riddled Panzer III was unsuited to street fighting, with insufficient armour and lacking a decent HE shell.

BELOW LEFT This is probably winter 1941, and shows 11th Panzer Division tanks and infantry near Wolokolamsk/Klin during the battle for Moscow. They wear no better winter clothing than greatcoats – some troops didn't even have them. The swastika flag was the standard German air recognition symbol.

BELOW An Ausf J with a lot of stowage on the engine decks, including enough wooden stools for the whole crew. Notice how the snow has packed into the roadwheels.

situation. No army can afford to lose over 300 tanks each month and receive only 22% of the replacements needed to make good those losses. As one commentator noted: 'New acquisitions were in no way able to compensate for the heavy losses of tanks suffered during the initial months of Barbarossa and never

replaced.' The lack of replacements would impact upon the order of battle: by 1942 a panzer division would have only one panzer battalion, rather than two full regiments.

Why was this so? Simply put, the *Panzerwaffe* had finally encountered an enemy that could cause them genuine problems and which led to them questioning the true battle worthiness of their tanks. A report said:

> At first only a few [Russian heavy tanks] appeared and could be driven off by concentrated artillery fire or bypassed. …
> After taking Orel [September–October 1941] the Russians employed their heavy tanks en masse for the first time. … For the first time during the campaign in the East the absolute superiority of the Russian T34 and KV tanks over our Panzer III and IV was felt. … The Russian tanks usually open fire with their 76.2mm guns on our Panzers at a range of 1000 meters and deliver enormous penetration energy with high accuracy. … Our 50mm KwK tank guns can achieve penetrations only on vulnerable locations under very favourable conditions at very close ranges.

This mismatch led to the Germans having to consider how best to counter the new threat, and turn this into practical advice for the crews to use. A German report in the summer of 1942

RIGHT Although the designers thought that the crews could avoid really muddy terrain, the Russian campaign proved this to be false, particularly during the spring thaw and when the rains fell. Note the open gunner's visor on the mantlet.

CENTRE Desperate times indeed with a 50mm-gunned Panzer III being used to recover a much lighter Panzer II. Although low temperatures caused huge problems when snow was lying on the ground, the thaw often made things even worse for the panzers, turning the ground into one huge bog, which made a mockery of the pre-war German doctrine of avoiding muddy areas. This photograph was taken in the early winter of 1941.
(Topfoto/Ullstein Bild)

issued instructions and advice for tank crews to use when fighting the T34. It stated that:

The T34 is faster and more manoeuvrable, has better cross country mobility than our Panzer III and IV. Its armour is stronger. The penetrative ability of its 7.62cm gun is superior to both the 5cm KwK38 and the 7.5cm KwK40. The design of the sloping armour plates assists in causing ricochets. Combating the T34 with the KwK38 tank gun is only possible at close ranges from the sides or from the rear, where it is important to strike it as close to perpendicular as possible. Strikes on the turret ring, using HE shells or even MG bullets, often result in jamming the turret. AP shells fired at close range and which hit the mantlet result in penetrations and cracking the weld seams. The T34 can be penetrated at ranges up to 1000m with the 75mm Hohlgranate *shells.*

The tank crews would doubtless have enjoyed being told to avoid hitting the enemy on the sloping armour, and to try to only hit it on

RIGHT Tanks used during the winter months had snow camouflage painted on them – sometimes over all surfaces, sometimes in a pattern. Chalk was even used.

a vertical surface – easier said than done. Equally, hitting a T34 with a low-velocity hollow charge shell at 1,000m, particularly if it was mobile, was no mean feat. The point about the better mobility of the Soviet tank is related directly to another German policy, formulated pre-war. It had been decided that cross-country mobility meant the ability to negotiate 'rough but firm' ground, and that heavy mud was to be avoided – this was clearly the experience of the First World War speaking. This made some sense if it could be guaranteed that the tanks would not have to fight in mud, but of course that was not so – the Russian conditions made muddy terrain a certainty, as heavy rains fell in the late autumn before the snows came, and the snow melted in the spring leaving a morass over the entire country which had few serviceable roads.

In March 1943 a panel of tank gunnery experts issued further instructions detailing the maximum ranges and aspects at which Panzer III crews could expect to penetrate the T34, for two types of ammunition. These have been converted into the two diagrams shown on page 148. It should be noted that due to the performance of the *PzGr* 40 falling

ABOVE AND BELOW A pair of images taken in the village of Matrenino west of Moscow in mid-November 1941. This advance was about as close as the Germans ever got to entering Moscow and represented the high tide of German success in 1941. These 37mm-armed tanks are taking part in Army Group Centre's push towards Klin, and include *Befehlspanzer* 001, a regimental commander. Note the distinctive striped winter camouflage pattern used by this unit, plus the additional – and much needed – extra stowage added on the engine decks. German troops suffered terrible hardships from the inability of the high command to supply them with adequate winter clothing, and the tanks frequently failed to cope with the extreme conditions. *(Topfoto/Ullstein Bild)*

ABOVE This Panzer III in Russia is using the specially designed *Ostketten* (Eastern tracks) with their very wide extensions; the spare track links are of the same type. Note the unusual position of spare roadwheels on the turret front.

RIGHT The 5th SS Panzer Division *Wiking* in action in Russia in the summer, where the heat and dust could be almost as unbearable as the cold of the Russian winter.

LEFT Two Panzer IIIs from 11th Panzer Division in Russia on the outskirts of Moscow; the distinctive Ghost insignia is painted on the rear of the hulls. Note that the crews are wearing greatcoats, which although the best items for keeping out some of the cold, were totally impractical within the confines of the tanks. German equipment and clothing, although much admired by post-war generations, often failed to meet the needs of the troops in combat.
(Topfoto/Ullstein Bild)

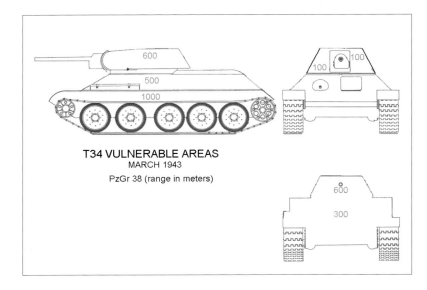

T34 VULNERABLE AREAS
MARCH 1943
PzGr 38 (range in meters)

600
500
1000
100 100
600
300

T34 VULNERABLE AREAS
MARCH 1943
PzGr 40 (range in meters)

500
400
600*
100 100
100
500
300

LEFT A 12th Panzer Division Ausf L fitted with the extended winter tracks.

off quickly after about 600m, the *PzGr 38* was often the better shell to use.

During the first winter, the average availability of tanks (expressed as a percentage of those battle worthy compared with the whole fleet) dropped from 80% at the start of winter to only 55% at its worst point. The Germans were better prepared for the winter of 1942/43, but even so the equivalent figures were 77% and 67%. It was obvious that specific measures and modifications were necessary to combat the effects of cold weather, and these were introduced from 1942 onwards in the form of wider tracks, engine and crew heating systems and the like. The gunner of a Panzer III, Oberschütze Kellermann wrote:

The cold has remained in my memory like a frozen nightmare ... the temperature often varied between fifteen and twenty five below zero. I recall one horrifying day of wind when it fell to thirty five below zero, and I thought I would die. Nothing could warm us. We urinated onto our numbed hands to warm them, and hopefully to cauterise the gaping cracks in our fingers.

Due to the mobility limitations of the PzKpw VI Tiger, Panzer IIIs were used in the Tiger battalions in a support function from 1942. Nine Tigers were issued to the first company of 502 *Schwere Panzer Abteilung* (heavy tank battalion) in August 1942; at the same time nine Panzer III Ausf Ls and nine Ausf Ns (straight from conversion) were issued to the unit, which was deployed to Russia in August 1942, the first operational deployment of the new heavy tank. We can assume that the unit followed German doctrine and that the Panzer Ausf Ns were in attendance when the first combat occurred in the middle of September near Leningrad.

A number of captured Panzer IIIs were supplied (in a rare example of co-operation from Stalin) to Britain in about 1942, allowing the British experts at the School of Tank Technology in Egham to examine models used on the Eastern Front, and compare them with the examples captured in North Africa. Aside

RIGHT Russian troops operating a Panzer III and two StuG IIIs. *(TM 18/B2)*

CENTRE A long-barrelled tank, probably an Ausf L, with the extended tracks on display, as well as numerous normal track links used as added armour. Oddly, it appears to have the early style of idler wheel fitted.

from the tropical changes used in Libya and the wider *winterketten* tracks and other cold weather modifications used in Russia, the tanks were found to be much the same – examining the equivalent tanks in service a year later might have shown more differences, as design changes to the Panzer III were led by the experience in the USSR, and in May 1943 the North African campaign had of course ended. The Russians did alert the British to the fitting of *Schürzen* from early 1943, which had not been encountered in North Africa, and which supports the conclusion that they were designed – initially at least – to counter a purely Russian threat.

Towards the end – Europe, 1943–45

After the end of the Tunisian campaign in May 1943, the next time that the British and Americans encountered the Panzer III was in Sicily and Italy later that year. Although the use of the Panzer III as the primary battle

LEFT A line of late-model Panzer IIIs in June 1943; interestingly, three have turret *Schürzen* fitted, but the hull plates have not been fitted and their mounting brackets appear to have been removed.

(Bundesarchiv)

ABOVE **The location of this tank has been variously described as Normandy and Arnhem. Whichever is correct, it has been penetrated at the junction of nose and glacis plates, as well as on the driver's visor, despite the appliqué armour. For some reason the steering brake air inlet cowls have been removed.**

Crusader. By 1944, though, the qualitative difference was more pronounced, and the Panzer III was outclassed by the 76mm-armed and up-armoured Shermans and of course by the Sherman Firefly. It continued to be used as a command tank, and in Italy the British encountered a number of *Flammpanzer III*, the first time that these had been deployed in Western Europe. In Normandy in 1944 the number of Panzer IIIs in service was likewise in decline but they were still being used. The 21st Pz Div (reconstituted after Africa) had three or four Ausf Ns and two *Befehlswagen*, and 116th Pz Div were still using 11 Panzer IIIs with the L/60 gun, by now hopelessly outclassed. *Befehlswagen* IIIs were also to be found in 9th SS (six), 10th SS (three) and 12th SS (two) Panzer Divisions, and three other gun tanks were recorded as being with other units. By way of comparison, at the same time there were 897 Panzer IVs used in the campaign, a clear picture of how the combat use of the tank had declined. One German veteran noted in his memoirs that there seemed to be a policy of putting the newer, less-experienced crews in the more capable Panthers and Tigers, leaving the experienced campaigners to man the older tanks; this is probably not a reflection of policy but it does beg the question just how confident the crew of a Panzer III would have felt by 1944.

tank was already on the decline, the Germans continued to use their remaining stocks as it still possessed reasonable qualities when compared to the early US Sherman or the British

RIGHT **A very rare image of a *Flammpanzer* III using its flame projector. This image appears to have been taken in Italy where a number of the *Flammpanzer* conversions were deployed. Additional stowage bins for the specialist equipment have been fitted on to the trackguards.** *(Bundesarchiv Bild 101I-306-0730-30)*

Use by other nations

Turkey

In 1942 it was decided to produce 56 Panzer IIIs (probably all Ausf Ms) for export to Turkey. Production took place in early 1943 at MNH, with numbers 76223 to 76278 allocated. It is not clear how many of them were actually shipped, as some at least were issued to German units, but there is a surviving Ausf M in the Etimesgut tank museum in Ankara. Why Germany, at that stage of the war, decided to send the equivalent of a strong tank regiment to a neutral country is not immediately clear, nor does it seem logical. It was all to do with political strategy rather than tactical necessity: Hitler was desperately trying to persuade Turkey (and in a similar vein Spain) to come into the war on Germany's side, and saw the provision of modern military equipment as part of the argument. Britain had negotiated arms supplies to the Turks but had decided to discontinue them in early 1942, presenting Hitler with an opportunity to demonstrate his support – guns, aircraft and submarines also formed part of the package. The perceived strategic effects were sufficiently compelling even at that desperate stage of the war, and in late 1943 Germany also shipped around 20 Panzer IVs to Spain for similar reasons. After the end of the war,

ABOVE One of the three Panzer IIIs used to train Polish troops on tanks in North Africa; note the British Red-White-Red recognition markings applied to the turret and hull. *(TM 2895/F2)*

both Norway and Denmark operated a number of Panzer IIIs for some years, from stocks surrendered by the Germans in May 1945. The Norwegians were still operating 32 as late as 1949. Other survivors were operated by Croatia, Hungary, Romania and Slovakia.

Three tanks – opinion differs as to the model, but they were probably Ausf Js – were captured in good condition at El Alamein in October 1942 and were passed to Polish forces in Egypt in

LEFT This is a very well-known and much reproduced image, purporting to show British troops capturing a Panzer III in action in 1942. However, careful examination reveals the Red-White-Red markings on the turret with the number 3, which tells us that this is one of the Polish-operated tanks and is really a posed propaganda photograph. *(Tank Museum)*

order to allow them to train on tanks. British markings were applied in the form of the Red-White-Red recognition rectangle on the turret sides, with the tank's number (1, 2 or 3).

Surviving tanks

Although at least 15 examples of the Panzer III survive in various conditions, it will come as no surprise that most of these are

late model tanks – Ausf Js and later. The earliest example appears to be the Ausf E in the Motor Technica Museum in Bad Oeynhausen, Germany. The Musée des Blindés in Saumur, France, holds an Ausf F, as does the Patton Museum in the USA. Kubina and Munsterlager both hold examples, and Aberdeen Proving Ground has two. The Bovington Tank Museum also has two: the restored Ausf L used extensively herein, and a cutaway Ausf N. For details of these plus others, please visit: preservedtanks.com

Let us conclude by looking at the human face of war, and in particular the careers of two German tank officers who knew the Panzer III intimately. Firstly, General Georg von Bismarck, a senior commander. He was born in 1881 and was a professional cavalry officer, fighting throughout the First World War. Having served in the Reichswehr, he was able to keep his career moving, commanding a mechanised reconnaissance battalion in 1934. He served in both Poland and France as a regimental commander, including as part of Rommel's 7th Pz Div in the latter campaign where he was awarded the Knight's Cross. He then took acting command of the 20th Pz Div in Russia in autumn 1941. He must have done well as

ABOVE **The Kubinka
Ausf L ...**

BELOW **... and the
Saumur Ausf F.**

ABOVE **A Panzer III owned by the RAF? Absolutely correct; this Ausf L survived until April 1953 when it was used by the RAF as a bombing target in Gütersloh.** *(TM 2382/E2)*

in January 1942 he was sent to North Africa to command 21st Pz Div – possibly on the direct recommendation of Rommel – and was promoted to major general in April. He was killed in action – variously reported as due to a mine, enemy air attack, or by mortar fire – at Alam el Halfa on 31 August 1942. He was buried at Tobruk.

Secondly, at the tactical level we meet the incredible Hans-Günther Stotten, who was born in 1916 and thus too young to have served in the First World War. He entered service in the newly proclaimed Wehrmacht as an 18-year-old, and joined Panzer Regiment 3. He served in Poland where he was decorated with the Iron Cross Second and First Classes, and was awarded the Knight's Cross in July 1940

RIGHT **The end of the road. This was the fate of many – or probably most – Panzer IIIs.**

OPPOSITE Many of the crews paid the ultimate price – Russia, August 1941.

for leading the 1st Company of Pz Regt 3 in France. In early 1941 he fought in the Greek campaign and then took part in Operation Barbarossa, being badly wounded during the advance on Moscow in late 1941. After he recovered he was posted to Panzer Regiment 8 in North Africa, firstly as a company and then as a battalion commander, where he fought in the Mareth and Alamein battles and then took over the regiment; Rommel is known to have rated him very highly. He commanded at Kasserine but was wounded again, which required him to be evacuated to Rome and then Germany. In May 1943 he was awarded the Oakleaves to the Knight's Cross and promoted to major. He later commanded a division and attended staff college, but was killed, aged 28, fighting the Russians at Wolfsgraben to the west of Vienna on 5 April 1945 – only a month before the end of a war in which he had taken part in all the major campaigns.

ABOVE Von Bismarck (front) observing operations with his Panzer III *Befehlswagen* alongside.

BELOW Stotten, pictured wearing the Oakleaves to his Knight's Cross (*Ritterkreuz*).

BELOW Stotten enjoying himself in action in North Africa – his Ausf N tank was pressed into service as a command vehicle and carried this distinctive marking on both sides. Note also the sandbags on the roof.

Chapter Seven

Restoring the Panzer III

The Tank Museum's early production Panzer III Ausf L was captured in North Africa in 1942 and acquired by the museum in 1951. Its restoration provides an unusual and revealing photographic record of the tank and its major systems.

OPPOSITE The turret of the Tank Museum's Panzer III is lifted from the vehicle using the Chieftain ARV.
(All photos Tank Museum)

As with many historic vehicles in museum collections, the Panzer III has gone through several paint schemes, mechanical tinkering and periods of static display and working demonstrations in its history. After a number of breakdowns and failures in the early 2000s, Mike Hayton of the Tank Museum workshops took charge of a restoration project which started with the investigation into some of the vehicle's problems. This led in turn to the disassembly of a number of key components and the investigation into the history of the paint schemes the tank sported. The tank still runs at special events at the museum and now looks much more as it would have done when captured in 1942.

The Tank Museum's example is an early production Ausf L, modified for 'tropical' service and stamped Tp or *Tropen* to indicate this. This tank was transported to Naples from the factory in Nuremburg by rail. It was shipped to Bengazi on the *Lerica*, arriving on 18 July 1942 as noted by the German port official. It was issued to the 8th Panzer Regiment as a replacement tank and brought the strength of the 15th Panzer Division up to 65 tanks by the beginning of August 1942. It arrived at the front between 28 and 31 July and so probably fought at the Battle of Alame Halfa, the last attempt by Rommel to break through the Eighth Army in the Western Desert. By 26 October the 15th Panzer Division had only 39 tanks left, after Montgomery refused to let his armoured formations leave their defensive positions, creating instead an impressive anti-tank position. Quite when the tank was captured is not clear – but images show it in a desert location before being sent to Britain for analysis.

The Panzer III was taken to Chertsey where evaluation of captured tanks was carried out during the Second World War. Here, images show the tank had an engine fire at some point during the evaluation process. From other examples of vehicles in the museum that were reassembled at Chertsey, not all parts were returned to the vehicle and sometimes major components from other

captured examples were mixed together – understandably preserving historical accuracy was not their priority.

The Panzer III came to the Tank Museum in 1951 and photographic evidence shows the vehicle being used at a number of museum events in a variety of paint schemes. As with many museum vehicles, the colour and markings of the Panzer III followed popular conventions of what was *believed* about German wartime vehicles – there was little accurate evidence published and scientific investigations of the vehicles and paint scrapes were in their infancy. The restoration of the Panzer III assisted Tom Jentz, the sadly missed doyen of German wartime tanks, in establishing the actual colours used at this period of production. These images show some of the work on the vehicle – and removed Panzer III components, pieces rarely seen off a vehicle.

ABOVE At some point during evaluation trials the engine appears to have suffered a fire – smoke damage and scorching can be seen on the rear of the hull. The removed engine decks are in the foreground inside the Chertsey hangar.

LEFT The tank arrived at Bovington in 1951. Here it can be seen with the museum's Sherman Crab.

RIGHT Looking up at the gun and turret roof, prior to restoration. The interior had been given a coat of brown paint at some point – but lettering on the turret interior had been masked.

FAR RIGHT Looking forward from the gunner's seat before restoration.

RIGHT Looking towards the rear of the fighting compartment showing an ammunition stowage locker.

BELOW The engine bay. On the right a section has been cut out of the fuel tank.

LEFT One of the ammunition stowage cabinets removed showing the Bakelite ammunition racks inside.

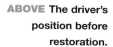

ABOVE The driver's position before restoration.

LEFT The stowage bin shows original paint on lid.

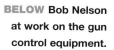

BELOW Bob Nelson at work on the gun control equipment.

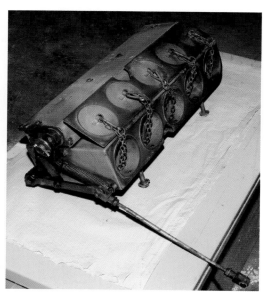

LEFT The smoke grenade dispenser removed for inspection.

ABOVE One of the commander's hatch covers in stripped condition.

ABOVE The commander's cupola being reassembled.

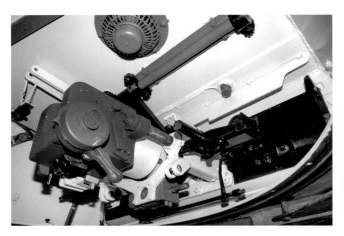

ABOVE The interior during restoration.

ABOVE RIGHT Tom Jentz and Mike Hayton look at the remaining original paint.

RIGHT The damaged front sprocket centre cap.

ABOVE Mike Hayton overseeing the fitting of the restored fan units.

RIGHT The recovered and restored driver's seat.

RIGHT The driver's position restored. Original paint is retained wherever possible.

BELOW The front hull machine-gun mount.

RIGHT The hull stripped down to bare metal and the original primer.

BELOW The turret is replaced.

KEEP OFF

LEFT The completed tank.

BELOW Panzer III '7' performs in Bovington's arena at Tank Fest 2015.

Appendix 1

Panzerkampfwagen III (SdKfz 141) – dimensions, capacities, details and data

Details refer to the specification of an 'average' mid-1942 tank in North Africa as examined by the AEC company and in other similar reports: changes, modifications and upgrades are covered within the text.

NOMENCLATURE	
Designation:	Panzerkampfwagen III *Ausfuhrung* G
DIMENSIONS	
Length (trackguards)	5.4m (17ft 9in)
Height (to top of commander's cupola)	2.52m (8ft 3in)
Width (trackguards)	2.93m (9ft 7in)
Track width	360mm (14½in)
Ground clearance	387mm (15¼in)
Mass (fully stowed but without crew or ammunition)	18,700kg (18 tons 10cwt)
Mass (fully laden)	19,400kg (19 tons 5cwt)
Crew	5
CAPACITIES	
Fuel	310 litres (72 gallons): minimum 72 octane
MOBILITY	
Maximum road speed	40kph (25mph)
Maximum reverse speed	5kph (3mph)
Vertical obstacle (step)	575mm (1ft 11in)
Maximum gradient	30°
Trench crossing	2.3m (7ft 6in)
Fording (unprepared)	800mm (2ft 7in)
Ground pressure	87 kilopascal (12.6lb/in^2)
Operating range	Road: 165km (102 miles); Cross-country: 95km (59 miles)
Engine	11.95 litre V-12 (60°) Maybach HL120 petrol engine
Bore	105mm
Stroke	115mm
Lubrication	Dry sump
Compression ratio	6.2:1
Firing order	1-12-5-8-3-10-6-7-2-11-4-9 (Nos 1 and 7 to rear of each bank)
Power	296bhp (300ps) @ 2,500rpm
Carburettor	Solex Twin Type 40 JFF2
Air cleaners	4 × oil-bath internal
Cooling	2 × radiators in hull rear with twin 21¾in fans, each 11-blade belt-driven @ 1.15 engine speed
Transmission	Maybach Variorex ten forward and four reverse gears, synchromesh

Steering	Epicyclic clutch brake principle, with Lockheed hydraulic control units
Final drive	Heavy spur gear 4:1 reduction
Suspension	12 torsion bars with shock absorbers front and rear
Electrical system:	12V lead acid 105ah batteries
	Bosch BNG4 5 24V electric starter (plus Bosch inertial manual starter)
	Bosch 50 (rated) 70 (max) amp dynamo
	Lights: head and side; tail; Notek combined convoy/tail
	Radio: FuG 5 transmitter/receiver with folding rod antenna

LETHALITY AND SURVIVABILITY

Armament:	5.0cm KwK 38 L/42 gun, firing AP, APC, APCBC and HE ammunition. 99 rounds carried in steel bins below turret ring. Elevation +20°, depression -10°. Turret ring 59¾in
	2 × MG42 with 3,750 rounds in 150-round belts. 2 × MP40, 1 × signal pistol
	30mm face-hardened armour basis. Welded hull and turret • 30mm Hull front and sidewalls, turret front, sides and rear, cupola incl. visors • 26mm Hull bottom front angled plate, hull front horizontal plate • 21mm Hull rear • 17mm Hull top and engine decks • 16mm Floor • 12mm Turret top
	5 × smoke grenades on rear hull, operated from within fighting compartment

KEY DOCUMENTATION

- AEC Report on examination of German tank type PZKW III, June 1942.
- Report on examination of the turret and armament: German PZKW III tank, August 1942.
- PzKpw III Ausf E *bis* J *Fritenheft*, July 1941.
- Maybach 12 *Zylinder-Vergassermotor Bauart* HL120TRM, February 1941.
- Panzerkampfwagen III: Notes on all types, including armament and ammunition.
- *Bildmappe Panzerkampwagen* III *Teil II Der Turm (Rheinmetall).*
- DTD PzKpw III Gearbox & Steering Unit.
- Examination of Welded Hull and Turret of German PzKpw III tank.
- Notes on the Wireless equipment of German tanks PzKpw III and IV.

Appendix 2

Abbreviations and glossary

Abteilung	Battalion
AP	Armour-piercing
APC	Armour-piercing capped
APCBC	Armour-piercing capped ballistic cap
APCR	Armour-piercing composite rigid
Ausf	*Ausfuhrung* (model)
Befehlspanzer	Command tank
Befehlswagen	Command vehicle
Benzin	Petrol
Beobachtungswagen	Observation vehicle
Bergepanzer	Recovery tank
Bugpanzer	Front armour (superstructure)
BW	*Battalionführerwagen* (battalion commander's vehicle) or *Begleitwagen* (support vehicle)
DAK	*Deutsches Afrika Korps*
Doppeltrommel	Double drum (MG magazine)
Drehsehklappe	Driver's vision visor (lit: pivoting vision flap)
Fahreroptik	Driver's periscope
Fahrersehklappe	Driver's vision flap
Fahrgestell	Chassis
Fahrgestellnummer	Chassis number
FH	Face-hardened (armour)
Flammpanzer	Flame (thrower) tank
Fu	Funk (radio)
FuG	*Funk Gerät* (radio set)
Führerprinzip	Leader principle (*ie* Hitler had the right, above law, to make all decisions)
HC	Hollow charge
HE	High-explosive
Heckpanzer	Rear armour (superstructure)
Heer	Army
Heereswaffenamt	Army Weapons Office
HF	High-frequency
Hohlgranate	Hollow charge shell (lit: hollow shell)
Ketten	Tracks (lit: chains)
Kriegsmarine	Navy
Kugelblende	Ball mounting (for MG)
KwK	*KampfWagenKanone* (combat vehicle cannon)
LK	*LeichtKampfWagen* (light combat vehicle)
Luftwaffe	Air Force
MG	*MaschinenGewehr* (machine gun)
MHz	Megahertz
Motor	Engine
MP	*Maschine pistole* (submachine gun)
mps	Metres per second
Munitionspanzer	Ammunition (carrying) tank
MW	Medium wave
Notek	Nova Technik
Ostketten	Eastern tracks
PaK	*PanzerAbwehrKanone* (anti-tank cannon)
Panzer	Armour
PanzerBefehlsWagen	Armoured command vehicle
Panzerbeobachtungswagen	Armoured observation vehicle
Panzertruppenschule	Tank training school
Panzerwaffe	Armoured forces
Prüfwesen	Testing
Pz Abt	*Panzer Abteilung* (battalion)
Pz Div	Panzer division
PzGr	*Panzergranate* (armour-piercing ammunition)
PzKpfw	*Panzerkampfwagen* (Armoured Combat Vehicle)
Pz Regt	Panzer regiment
Rahmenantenne	Frame antenna
Reichswehr	Armed forces (pre-1933)
RHA	Rolled homogenous armour
RM	Reichsmark
Schürzen	Armour skirts on the hull and/or turret (lit: aprons)
Schutzglaser	Armoured glass prism (lit: protective glass)
Schwere Panzer Abteilung	Heavy tank battalion
SdKfz	*Sonderkraftfahrzeug* (special purpose vehicle)
SmK	AP ammunition (small arms)
SmK (L'spur)	AP ammunition with tracer (small arms)
Sperrverband	Blocking detachment
Sprengpatrone	HE cartridge
SprGr	*Sprenggranate* (HE shell)
sS	Ball ammunition (small arms)
Sternantenne	Star antenna
Sturmgeschutz	Assault gun
Tauchpanzer	Diving tank
Tornister	Backpack (radio)
Truppenamt	Troop office
VK	*Versuchtkraftfahrzeug* (experimental vehicle)
Vorpanzer	Forward armour (spaced appliqué)
Waffenamt	Weapons Office
Wehrmacht	Armed forces (post-1933)
Winterketten	Winter tracks
Zusatzpanzerung	Additional armour
ZW	*Zugführerwagen* (platoon commander's vehicle)

Bibliography

Anon, *Notes on the Wireless Equipment of Panzer III & IV* (Official, 1945)

Anon, *Illustrated Record of German Army Equipment Vols II and III* (NMP, 2004)

Atkinson, Rick, *An Army at Dawn* (Abacus, 2003)

Bance, Alan (Trans), *Blitzkrieg in Their Own Words* (Pen & Sword, 2005)

Barr, Niall and Hart, Russell, *Panzer* (Aurum Press, 1999)

Brendon, Piers, *The Dark Valley* (Pimlico, 2001)

British Intelligence Objectives Sub-Committee Reports (Official, 1945) (various)

Citino, Robert M., *The Path to Blitzkrieg* (Stackpole, 1999)

Clark, Alan, *Barbarossa* (Cassell, 2005)

Combined Intelligence Objectives Sub-Committee Reports (Official, 1945) (various)

Corum, James, *The Roots of Blitzkrieg* (UP Kansas, 1992)

Deist, Wilhelm et al., *Germany and the Second World War* (Clarendon, 1990)

Evans, Richard J., *The Third Reich in Power* (Penguin, 2005)

Freidli, Lukas, *Repairing the Panzers Vols I and II* (Panzerwrecks, 2011)

Frieser, Karl-Heinz, *The Blitzkrieg Legend* (MGFA, 2005)

Gander, Terry, *Tanks in Detail 7, PzKpw III* (Ian Allan, 2003)

Guderian, Heinz, *Achtung – Panzer!* (Cassell, 1992)

Guderian, Heinz, *Panzer Leader* (Penguin, 1996)

Healy, Mark, *Camouflage & Markings Vol 1* (SAM, 2013)

Hoffschmidt, E.J. and Tantum, W.H., *German Tank and Anti-tank* (WE Inc., 1968)

Irving, David, *The War Path* (Macmillan, 1983)

Irving, David, *Hitler's War Vols 1 and 2* (Macmillan, 1983)

Jentz, Thomas, *Panzer Truppen Vols 1 and 2* (Schiffer, 1996)

Jentz, Thomas, *Tank Combat in North Africa* (Schiffer, 1998)

Jentz, Thomas and Doyle, Hilary, *Panzer Tracts* Nos 3.1 to 3.5, 23 (Panzer Tracts, various years)

Johannis, Eberhard, *Amphibious Tanks* (Trans. Cpt Norbert Brandon) (Armor, Jan–Feb 1959)

Kitchen, Martin, *Rommel's Desert War* (Cambridge University Press, 2009)

Lucke, Fritz, *Panzer Wedge Vols 1 and 2* (Stackpole, 2012, 2013)

Macmillan, Margaret, *Peacemakers* (John Murray, 2003)

Mosier, John *The Blitzkrieg Myth* (HarperCollins, 2003)

Overy, Richard, *The Road to War* (Penguin, 1999)

Ripley, Tim, *Steel Storm* (Sutton, 2000)

Smithers, A.J., *Rude Mechanicals* (Grafton, 1989)

Speer, Albert, *Inside the Third Reich* (Phoenix, 1995)

Spielberger, Walter, *Panzer III and its Variants* (Schiffer, 1993)

Stolfi, R.H.S., *Hitler's Panzers East* (Oklahoma University Press, 1991)

Tirone, Laurent, *Panzer: The German Tanks Encyclopaedia* (Caraktère, 2015)

Von Mellenthin, F.W., *Panzer Battles* (Norman, 1956)

Index